SOME OF THE SIX HUNDRED

JAMES W BANCROFT

JWB

Published in 2007 by **J W B**
280 Liverpool Road, Eccles M30 0RZ, England
Telephone: 0161 707 6455

ISBN: 978-0-9555983-1-9

Edited by James W Bancroft
Designed and Produced by John Bancroft
Artwork by Tracey Bancroft

CONTENTS

Acknowledgements

I would like to acknowledge the help of the late Canon William Lummis, James Boys and David Harvey, with whom I exchanged information concerning Light Brigade men for many years, and the regimental museums of the five cavalry regiments involved. Many descendants of Light Brigade men and people who own their medals kindly offered information, and I am most grateful to Kris Wheatley, whose work in researching census returns and other official documentation has been invaluable.

THE CRIMEAN WAR

By the middle of the nineteenth century the Turkish Ottoman Empire was falling apart, and Britain and France were suspicious of Russia's expansionist intentions in the Balkans. This was inflamed when Tsar Nicholas began to interfere in Turkish affairs, and the Sultan appealed to Britain and France for guidance. However, there was a lack of co-operation on both sides, and Turkey declared war on Russia in October 1853. Russian forces destroyed a Turkish fleet in the following month, which caused a wave of hostility. Diplomacy broke down, and by March 1854 Britain had drifted into war.

An Allied Anglo-French expeditionary force was sent to the East, which arrived at Varna in Bulgaria in the Summer of 1854. But as they waited for orders to proceed their numbers were seriously depleted by the ravages of a cholera epidemic. The Crimea was invaded in September 1854, the objective being to attack the strategic Black Sea port of Sebastopol. On 20 September the first battle was fought at the river Alma. The Russians had entrenched themselves on high ground and the British were in the fore of a frontal attack which broke them and drove them back. But the Allies did not follow up the victory and gave the Russians time to secure themselves in Sebastopol.

The British made their base camp at Balaclava, about ten miles south-east of Sebastopol, and on the morning of 25 October the Russians launched an offensive from the north-east towards the harbour. After driving Turkish troops out of a number of redoubts and capturing some British naval guns, they were stopped by Col Campbell's 93rd Highlanders, and driven back by the Charge of the Heavy Brigade. Later Lord Cardigan led the ill-fated Light Brigade into the annals of British military history. On 5 November 1854, the 'Soldiers' Battle' was fought among mist and fog at Inkerman. After seven hours of fierce fighting, over ten thousand men had been killed or wounded.

Bad planning and inefficiency had resulted in inadequate supplies. Medical attention was minimal, and the hospital at Scutari was disorganised and filthy. On the same day as the battle of Inkerman, Florence Nightingale and her complement of dedicated nurses arrived to eventually bring some comfort and cleanliness to the wounded. However, undernourished British troops continued to suffer in the harsh Crimean winter.

After six bombardments and two costly assaults on a Sebastopol strong-point called The Redan, made on 18 June and September 1855, the Russians evacuated the city. The war was brought to an unsatisfactory end by the Treaty of Paris in February 1856. The first one hundred and eleven Victoria Crosses were awarded for the campaign, and Roger Fenton's photographs were the first ever to be taken in a war zone.

BALACLAVA

was mid-morning at Balaclava, on Wednesday, 25 October 1854, as Lord Raglan looked east from his vantage point on the Sepoune Heights, where he had a panoramic view of the battlefield. The plain, six hundred feet below him, was divided into a north and south valley by the Causeway Heights, which carried the main track up to the plateau, and where the British had built six redoubts, installed some naval guns, and manned them with Turkish troops. Behind him to the west, Allied forces were laying siege on Sebastopol.

At dawn that day the Russians had made a threatening advance towards the harbour at Balaclava; only two miles south of the Causeway. After an hour Turkish troops had fled from the redoubts, leaving British naval guns behind, and the Russians occupied the three most easterly. A large force of Russian cavalry entered the south valley and four squadrons broke off making directly for Balaclava. Suddenly, a 'Thin Red Line' of 93rd Highlanders, led by Colin Campbell, appeared from behind a hill and blocked their way. Volley fire from the Highlanders checked the Russian advance and unnerved them, and they were soon put in reverse. Then Sir James Scarlett led eight hundred men of his Heavy Brigade at the main body of enemy horsemen. They ploughed into the stunned Russians, smashing and cutting at them until they broke and fled back over the Causeway, desperately trying to reform at the eastern end of the north valley.

All this time Lord Cardigan, commanding the British Light Cavalry, had been seated on his charger in front of his Brigade, which he had kept standing to horses in ranks across the end of the north valley below the Sepoune Heights, and the men were becoming frustrated with being deliberately held back. The 11th Hussars, 13th Light Dragoons and 17th Lancers formed the front line of the Brigade, while the second line consisted of the 4th Light Dragoons and the 8th Hussars. His officers had urged him to allow them to attack the flank of the retreating Russians, but Cardigan would take nothing from his subordinates and refused. About six hundred and seventy Light Cavalrymen were on duty. They had taken little part in the battle so far, and they were furious that 'The finest cavalry brigade that ever left the shores of England', had not been used in an independent action.

At his observation post Lord Raglan had his attention brought to the distant high ground where there seemed to be movement in the redoubts, and it was suggested that the Russians were limbering up the British naval guns to take them away. This was the equivalent of an infantry regiment losing their colours and he was alarmed. He wrote a hasty note, and gave it to Captain Nolan, 15th Hussars, to take to Lord Lucan, the cavalry commander. Nolan was a cavalry fanatic, who was agitated by the inaction of the Light Brigade. But he was a good horseman, and he arrived safely with the message.

Lord Lucan was sitting on his horse between the two Brigades. Nolan had little respect for the senior officer who he had nicknamed 'Lord Look-on!' and he thrust the note at him. Lucan opened it and read: *"Lord Raglan wishes the cavalry to advance rapidly to the front, follow the enemy, and try to prevent the enemy carrying away the guns. Troop Horse Artillery may accompany. French cavalry is on your left. Immediate."*

Lord Lucan did not have the extensive range of view that Lord Raglan had up on the ridge. He could see no significant enemy activity, except in the distance at the far end of the valley, where an eight gun Russian battery was situated, and he was bewildered by the order. Nolan impatiently urged him to attack, but Lucan retorted angrily, 'Attack, Sir! Attack what? What guns, sir?' Nolan pointed eastward, and replied sharply, 'There, my Lord, is your enemy; there are your guns.' Lord Lucan shrugged his shoulders. It would seem that he must order the Light Brigade to attack the Russian guns at the other end of the valley. He cantered towards Lord Cardigan, while Nolan took up a position in front of the 17th Lancers, fully intending to take part in the action.

Lord Lucan and Lord Cardigan were brothers-in-law and disliked each other. But on hearing the orders, Cardigan maintained courtesy, and remarked, 'Certainly, sir, but allow me to point out to you that the Russians have a battery in the valley to our front, and batteries and riflemen on each side!' Lord Lucan shrugged his shoulders again, and reminded Lord Cardigan that they had no choice but to obey. Cardigan

brought down his sword in salute, wheel his horse about and turned to the Brigad muttering, 'Well, here goes the last of t Brudenells.' He took his place ahead of h men, and at about ten minutes past eleve he gave the order, 'The Brigade wi advance. Walk march, trot.' The 11 Hussars dropped back, and they move down the valley in three lines, two hundre yards across and four hundred yards apart

As the pace quickened the first Russian ba rage thundered across the valley. At th same time Captain Nolan spurred his hors forward, and galloped across the advancin line from left to right, with his sword wav ing in the air. He was seen to turn and shou back, just before a shell burst close to him A piece of metal ripped into his chest an tore it apart. He gave out a terrible cry, an his horse bolted with his body trapped i the saddle. He was dragged for a consider able distance before he fell to the ground.

The Brigade broke into a gallop as the came into a dreadful shower of shot an shell from the Russian guns that were situ ated to the right on the Causeway Heights and to the front of them at the end of th valley. Still Lord Cardigan, rigidly facin ahead, led them forward through the heav acrid smoke and the dust kicked up by thei horses' hooves. The roar of cannon wa deafening, and there was a continuou whine of musket-balls in the air. Russia shells ripped up the ground, sending mer and horses sprawling over each other Limbs were torn from bodies, heads blowr from shoulders and there was a horribl thud and slush as groups of troopers were blasted out of existence. Men struggled to free themselves from beneath their fallen

'All That Was Left Of Them'

This famous painting of cavalrymen returning from the charge of the Light Brigade was produced the year after the first Balaclava reunion banquet. The artist, Lady Butler, took great care over details, and several survivors who posed for her appear in the picture. The original painting is housed at the Manchester City Art Gallery.

horses, or writhed in agony among the carnage left behind as the wave of British cavalry, their adrenaline in full flow, raced forward. The brigade began to take echelon shape, and as the shocked onlookers began to realise Lord Cardigan's objective, the French general, Bosquet, remarked emotionally: 'It is magnificent, but it is not war. It is madness.' They were almost at the Russian battery when a cannonade from almost all the guns at once almost annihilate the front line.

The Russian drivers tried to limber-up the guns to get them away as the British plunged headlong in at them. The momentum of the pace took the leading rank right through the line of enemy guns and into the stunned Russian cavalry standing to horses at the rear. The 4th Light Dragoons and the 11th Hussars then came in and engaged the Artillerymen, while the 8th Hussars veered to the right in order to take them in the flank and rear. A desperate hand-to-hand struggle ensued.

The panic-stricken Russian gunners tried to defend their field pieces by fending off the attackers with their rammers, but flashing British sabres cut many of them down, hacking mercilessly at those who tried to get away. The Brits had quite a free hand for several minutes, during which time they spiked the guns. They were attempting to try to pull some away when the officers saw that the enemy cavalry were re-forming, so the call to rally was sounded. Some troopers managed to locate each other amid the gun-smoke and re-formed in groups, but they found the way back blocked by a body of Russian Lancers who had ridden down from the hillside. Sections of British horsemen were brought into formation, wheeled about and charged. Once again Russian nerve failed against British grit, and the Light Brigade broke them.

The survivors were still in great danger, and it was every man for himself as they tried to get back to the British lines. Russian artillerymen had returned to their cannon and riflemen sent volleys up the valley, bringing down horses and men as they tried to get out of range. At the same time they were in danger from the Cossacks who had moved in to pillage the dead and finish off the wounded. Other survivors were taken prisoner. The Russian battery and riflemen on the hills opened fire again, but an attack by the French horsemen of the 4th Chasseurs d'Afrique put them out of action. At last the blood-spattered remnants of the Light Brigade began to get back from the mouth of hell, many of them terribly maimed.

Lord Cardigan addressed fewer than two hundred men that managed to answer the roll call, with the promise: 'Men you have done a glorious deed. England will be proud of you, and grateful to you. If you live to get home, be sure you will be provided for. Not one of you fellows will have to seek refuge in a workhouse.' The final casualty list was believed to be a hundred and thirteen killed and a hundred and thirty-four wounded, with the loss of four hundred and seventy five horses.

The Light Brigade action at Balaclava w ill-fated before it began, and had little eff on the outcome of the battle. Howev contrary to popular belief the men who to part were proud of what they had achieve and would have done it again had they be ordered to do so. It had a devastating eff on the enemy cavalry, who were relucta to face the British for the rest of the co flict, and it is still considered by many be, as Lord Raglan was to state later - 'T finest thing ever done.'

On 25 October 1875, a Balaclava reuni banquet was held at the Alexandra Palace London, and from it a Balacla Commemoration Society was formed 1877, which in 1879 restricted its membe to those who had taken part in the Lig Brigade action at Balaclava. On the occ sion of Queen Victoria's Golden Jubilee 1887, the survivors signed a Loyal Addre which was presented to her.

In 1897, T Harrison Roberts, a Londo journalist and publisher, invited seventy three survivors to an all-expenses-paid vis to his offices in Fleet Street to watch th Diamond Jubilee procession on 22 Jun Queen Victoria stopped her carriage t acknowledge the party of proud veteran. Mr Roberts was shocked to learn that man of them lived in poverty and he decided t start a public fund. Survivors received weekly pension from the fund, and n recipient of the T H Roberts Relief Fun had need to enter a workhouse or have paupers burial. On 25 October 1890 a Annual Dinner was held at the Alexandr Palace, and these continued on the anniver sary of the battle until 1913, by which tim there were few survivors left.

The first Dragoon regiment was raised in 1645 for service in Oliver Cromwell's 'New Model Army', to fight for the Parliamentarian cause in the English Civil War. They took their name from the matchlock carbine weapon they used - the dragon - so called because of the dragon's head emblem on the muzzle.

Dragoons were originally mounted infantry trained to fight on foot. The horse's only function being to transport the soldier to a place where he could dismount and reinforce the regular infantry. Some Dragoon regiments were adopted for scouting duties, using small men carrying light equipment. These units came to be recognised as elite troops paid at a higher rate than foot soldiers. The five regiments which formed the Light Brigade at Balaclava had fought with distinction for over a hundred years prior to the Crimea, in the British Army's many campaigns at home and overseas.

4th Light Dragoons
(Queen's Own)

Colonel John Berkeley had fought with distinction at the battle of Sedgemoor in 1685, and was commissioned to form and command a regiment of Dragoons from the Wessex area. They took the name The Princess Anne of Denmark's Regiment of Dragoons in honour of King James II's daughter. They were more commonly known as Berkeley's Dragoons.

Battle honours prior to the Crimea were gained at Dettingen 1743, during the war of the Austrian Succession; and for their part in the Peninsular War they gained battle honours for Talavera 1809, Albuhera 1811, Salamanca 1812, Vittoria 1813, Toulouse 1814, and Peninsula 1809-14. While serving in India they provided units for the expedition to Afghanistan, gaining battle honours for the storming of Ghuznee 1839, and Afghanistan 1838-39.

The regimental colours are blue with yellow busby bag. The motto in English is *With Heart And Hand*, and their nickname is 'Paget's Irregular Horse'. At the battle of Balaclava they were commanded by Lord George Paget, who was second in command of the Brigade.

8th Hussars
(King's Royal Irish)

After the War of the English Succession, William of Orange desired to raise a regiment of loyal Irish protestants who had fought at the battle of the Boyne in 1690. Command was given to Lt-Colonel Henry Cunyngham, who had fought at the Boyne with his father's regiment, the Inniskilling Dragoons. The new unit took the name Cunyngham's Regiment of Irish Dragoons.

Battle honours prior to the Crimea were gained while they were serving in India from 1802 to 1822; at Leswaree and Hindustan 1803.

The colours of the regiment are blue with scarlet busby bag, and their motto in English is *I Serve*. During the battle of Saragossa in 1710 they captured a unit of Spanish Horse and appropriated their belts, from which came the inspiration for their nickname 'The Cross Belts'. At the battle of Balaclava they were commanded by Lt-Colonel Frederick Shewell.

11th Hussars
(Prince Albert's Own)

Brigadier-General Philip Honywood raised a regiment of Dragoons in the Essex area at the time of the Jacobite Rebellion in 1715. He is believed to have originally mounted them on grey horses.

Battle honours prior to the Crimea were gained during the Seven Years War in Germany 1760-63, and in Flanders 1793-95, at Warburg, Beaumont and Willems. The battle honour Egypt (with the Sphynx) was gained in 1801. During the Peninsular War they gained honours at Salamanca 1812, and Peninsula 1811-13. They served in India from 1819 to 1838, gaining honours during the siege of Bhurtpore in 1825.

Their colours are blue with crimson busby bag, and the 11th Hussars overalls (trousers) are also crimson, a unique distinction authorised by Queen Victoria in recognition that the regiment escorted Prince Albert to the royal wedding in 1840. This also gave them their nickname 'The Cherrybums', and their motto in English is *Staunch and Steadfast*. At the battle of Balaclava they were commanded by Lt-Colonel John Douglas.

13th Light Dragoons

The 13th Light Dragoons were raised in the Midlands by Brigadier-General Richard Munden, at the time of the Jacobite Rebellion of 1715.

Battle honours prior to the Crimea were gained in the Peninsular War at Albuhera 1811, Vittoria 1813, Orthes 1814, Toulouse 1814, and Peninsula 1811-14. They also gained the honour for the battle of Waterloo 1815.

The colours of the Regiment are blue with buff collars, and their motto in English is *It Flourishes For Ever*. Their nickname is 'The Green Dragoons' or 'Evergreens'. At the battle of Balaclava they were commanded by Captain John Oldham, who was killed in action.

17th Lancers
(Duke of Cambridge's Own)

Raised in 1759 by Colonel John Hale, as the 18th Light Dragoons, they were re-designated the 17th Light Dragoons in 1763, and when Lancer units came into the British Army after the battle of Waterloo they replaced the 19th Light Dragoons as the 17th Lancers in 1822.

Their colours are dark blue with white facings. Colonel Hale devised the unique 'death's head' badge emblem, and the motto *Or Glory*, hence the famous nickname 'The Death Or Glory Boys'. At the battle of Balaclava they were commanded by the 'Pocket Hercules' Captain William Morris.

UNIFORMS AND WEAPONS

Light Dragoons

At the time of the Crimean War the headress of Light Dragoons was a black beaver shaco. They wore a dark blue double-breasted tunic which was decorated with gilt and gold chord. The dark blue overalls (trousers) had two gold lace stripes down the outer seam which indicated that they were light cavalry. However, in the Crimea the 13th were wearing experimental grey trousers. The overalls were pocketless, so the trooper carried a sabretache, which was an embroidered hanging pouch attached to the sabre belt. These had been discarded for the Crimean campaign. All light cavalry units wore the less bulky ankle boots.

Hussars

Hussar uniforms generally consisted of a scarlet busby cap, with white plume and red busby bag. Blue-cloth single-breasted jackets were laced and ornamented across the chest with braid. They wore a scarlet waistcoat, and a blue-cloth pelisse (hanging jacket) draped over the left shoulder. When worn, the sabretache was of scarlet embroidered cloth. Hussar units wore blue overalls (except the 11th), and had blue facings.

Lancers

The 17th Lancers wore a dark blue double breasted jacket and dark blue overalls. However, like the Light Dragoons they were wearing grey trousers in the Crimea. Their headress was the truncated lancer cap, which was white like their facings. In foul weather they wore a black covering over the helmet.

Weapons

At the time of the Crimean War Light Cavalry carried a steel sword, and 'other ranks' were issued with percussion carbines. Officers carried revolvers, while Troop Sergeant-Majors, trumpeters and Lancers used pistols. Lancers also carried a staff which was nine feet long and made of ash wood. A red and white pennon was attached close to the pointed steel head.

FREDERICK THOMAS ARMES
4TH *LIGHT DRAGOONS*

Fred Armes was born in 1831, at Dove Lane, Norwich, one of six sons to a leather cutter. He was an apprentice to the leather business, but he wanted to travel and left Norwich at an early age. In 1852 he returned to his home town where the 4th Light Dragoons were stationed, and enlisted into that regiment.

He received orders for active service in the Crimea and embarked on the *Simla* at Devonport, on 16 July 1854. He took with him a bible which had been presented to him by the ladies of Totnes two days before he left. He carried the bible in his holster during the battle of the Alma but lost it. The bloodstained book was returned to him years later by a soldier who had picked it up off the battlefield. During the battle he remembered seeing some Russian 'gentlemen and ladies' in carriages on the heights watching the British advance, and saw them running "as fast as legs could carry them" to get out of range when the Russians retreated.

He was promoted to corporal on the eve of Balaclava, but it had not been confirmed when he went into battle. During the Light Brigade action, a shell exploded and wounded his horse, and he received a wound in his hand, which caused the loss of one of his fingers. He was told to fall back and have the injury attended to, but he chose to remain with his comrades, and when he reached the Russian battery his spirited horse leapt over a gun and carried him into the thick of the fighting. While returning up the valley he received a serious wound from a round of shot which knocked him to the ground and his mount at last collapsed from injury and exhaustion. As he lay helpless on the floor a Cossack ran a lance into his leg and broke it. Dangerously wounded, he was taken to Scutari Hospital where he was nursed by Florence Nightingale, and Miss Stanley, daughter of the ex-Bishop of Norwich. He was invalided back to Netley Hospital, where he was visited by Queen Victoria, who placed a silk scarf around his neck. He was discharged with a small pension, and a Crimea Medal with *Alma, Balaclava* and *Sebastopol* clasps and the Turkish Medal.

He returned to Norwich, where he became bugle-major with the 1st Norfolk Volunteers carrying out his duties to the letter; and he taught at the St Peter Mancroft Sunday School. For recreation he was a good musician, and a keen amateur painter, giving many landscapes away to his friends. He attended the Balaclava reunion banquet in 1875, and was a member of the Commemoration Society.

He died at his home in All Saint's Green Norwich, on 21 January 1885, aged fifty-four. His impressive funeral was attended by many local dignitaries and military units, and thousands of people lined the streets as the cortege made its way for burial with military honours at the Rosary Cemetery. The scarf the Queen had presented to him was placed around his neck, and his shako and sword were carried on the coffin.

WILLIAM BENTLEY
11TH HUSSARS

William Bentley was born at Kilnwick-on-the-Wolds, a village near Driffield in the North Riding of Yorkshire, on 25 October 1816, a date which was to have great significance on his life. He came from a farming family, and some of his descendants still farm in the Yorkshire dales.

William enlisted into the 11th Hussars at Beverley in Yorkshire, on 7 July 1835, at the age of nineteen, and he was on duty with the troops who escorted Prince Albert to London for his marriage to Queen Victoria. He himself married at about this time, his new wife being called Mary, and their first child, Mary, was baptised in the chapel of the Royal Hospital, Kilmainham, Dublin, on 30 July 1843. He was promoted corporal on 30 June 1851, and sergeant on 15 November 1853. He sailed with the regiment for active service in the East, taking part in the Light Brigade action at Balaclava on his birthday.

As the exhausted survivors were returning to the British lines some horse began to slow down with fatigue. Cossacks moved in on the stragglers, and Sergeant Bentley, with fellow Yorkshireman Private Robert Levett, were hotly pursued and attacked from behind. As they struggled to escape an enemy bullet grazed Bentley's calf and a lance prod to the back of his neck knocked him from his mount. Bentley retained his weapon and retaliated by thrashing an officer across his face with his sword, but both he and Levett were in grave danger.

Some officers saw their plight and dropped back to assist. One of them being a dashing young man named Alexander Dunn, who had acquired a sword which was much larger than the regulation. He attacked the enemy cavalrymen on his frenzied charger, and wielding this powerful weapon he hacked and slashed at them, cutting them down with gallant determination. Sergeant Bentley escaped bur Private Levett was killed.

For his service in the East, Sergeant Bentley received the Crimea Medal with *Alma, Balaclava, Inkerman* and *Sebastopol* clasps and the Turkish Medal. Lieutenant Dunn was awarded the Victoria Cross for his valour.

The Hussar units smash their way through the Russian guns.

William was promoted to Sergeant-Major in E Troop on 26 November 1855. He discharged from the army at Birmingham on 7 July 1860, having served for over twenty-five years. His discharge papers state that he was aged forty-four, was five feet eight-and-a-half inches tall, with a fresh complexion, brown hair and hazel eyes. His character was described as 'very good', and he was never court-martialled.

His intended place of residence was given as the Royal Witshire Yeomanry at Calne, and he served with that unit as drill instructor for twelve years. His wife died on 28 January1883, at 63 Lowther Street, Groves, York. When he retired in 1884 he had been in military service for thirty-seven years. He had three daughters, and four sons who also chose the forces as a career. When his medals came up for sale at Glendinings auctioneers in 1968 the lot included an

Ashanti Medal, 1873-74, to Bandsm[a] George Bentley, *HMS Rattlesnake*; an Indi[a] General Service Medal, with a *Perak 18[?]* clasp, to 2099 Private Thomas Bentle[y] 1st/3rd Regiment; and an Egyptian Med[al] 1882, with a *Tel-el-Kebir* clasp, to Priva[te] Francis Bentley, 15th Company, Supply a[nd] Transport Corps.

He was present at the first Balaclava reuni[on] banquet in 1875, was a member of t[he] Balaclava Commemoration Society, and [he] signed the Loyal Address.

After a long and painful illness, Willia[m] Bentley died at his home, 2 St John['s] Crescent, Penley's Grove Street, York, on [?] March 1891, aged seventy-four. He wa[s] buried at York Cemetery, with military hon[o]ours provided by the 10th Hussars. Joh[n] Hogan and William Pearson attended th[e] funeral.

JAMES BOLTON
4TH *LIGHT DRAGOONS*

James Bolton was born at Gillingham in Kent in 1813, the son of John Bolton. He was employed as a servant prior to enlisting into the 4th Light Dragoons on 24 March 1837. He sailed with the regiment for active service in the East, and he was sick at Scutari until 4 October 1854. He took part in the Light Brigade action at Balaclava, where he was captured by the Russians.

Another prisoner stated: "We were very roughly used. The Cossacks at first hauled us along by the tails of our coatees and our haversacks. When we got on foot they drove their lance butts into our backs to stir us on.

When we reached the Tchernaya the Russians were as kind to us as the Cossacks had been brutal before. We found there a number of comrades; for some of us water was fetched, to others was given vodka. We were soon conveyed in bullock carts to a village a little distance in rear, where our wounds were attended to.

General Liprandi, the Russian commander, was so good as to pay us a visit. He was very pleasant, and spoke excellent English. 'Come now, men,' he asked, 'what did they give you to drink? Did they not prime you with spirits to come down and attack us in such a manner?"

Sergeant-Major William Fowler of James's regiment, who was severely wounded and died later, struggled to his feet to stand to attention and salute the general, and replied: 'On my honour, sir, there is not a man who has tasted food or drink this day.' Liprandi was moved. As he was leaving he informed them that the Light Brigade had lost over four hundred horses, denounced the charge as 'sheer madness,' but said that they were 'noble fellows.'" Private Bolton spent a year in enemy hands at Simferopol, before being liberated at an exchange of prisoners. For his service he received the Crimea Medal with *Alma, Balaclava* and *Sebastopol* clasps.

On his return to England he served at various stations, including Coventry, where a child named John was born in 1859. James Bolton discharged from the army soon after his second son, James, was born in Dublin in 1862.

He took his family to live in the village of Wheldrake, near York, where William was born in 1863, and Robert was born in 1865. After the death of his wife, James moved his family to the city of York, making their home at 79 Main Street, Gate Fulford. The 1871 census describes him as a fifty-eight year old pensioner, and also at the address is a twenty-one year old York-born servant girl named Ellen Frankish.

James attended the 1875 Balaclava reunion banquet, and had just become a member of the Balaclava Commemoration Society when he died at his home on 17 April 1879, aged sixty-six. He was buried in York Cemetery (grave 12803). There is no memorial stone.

RICHARD BROWN
11TH HUSSARS

Richard Brown was born at Wrighton, near Malton, North Yorkshire, in May 1825. He was the son of a farmer, and worked as a rural labourer until he enlisted into the 11th Hussars at York on 19 April 1843. In an account published in 1890 he was described as: 'Nearly sixty-five years of age, but doesn't look fifty. Still a fine handsome fellow, six feet in his stockings. No kink in his back or stoop in his shoulders yet; hair hardly changing colour, moustache turning grey at the tips, eyes full of fire, and the whole frame surcharged with vitality.'

In 1902 Private Pennington said of him: 'He had been the favourite orderly of Lord Cardigan, and was for some years the devoted and trusty henchman of Colonel Douglas. Handsome and honest, he was truly a model soldier, for, in his long service of 21 years he was never in the defaulters book. It was known that if he had not been illiterate he would have borne Her Majesty's commission'.

In the 1890 account he continued: 'I did most of my early soldiering in Dublin. I was amongst the detachment that broke up Dan O'Connell's repeal meeting the day before he was arrested and taken to Kilmainham (Prison). The boys came down in thousands with scythes and sickles and long poles that Sunday morning, but there was no fighting, and right glad we were about it too'.

He set sail to the East from Kingstown, Ireland, aboard the *War Cloud* as servant to

his Commanding Officer, Colonel John Douglas. He took part in the Light Brigade action at Balaclava. His account states: '...we were on the gunners and all over them. My horse went down wallop, his near fore-leg cut clean off with a twenty-four pounder at close range. I fell on one artilleryman, cut another's arm off as he raised his rammer at me, and lifted the roof off another one's head. Poor devils! ...Then two mounted Cossacks attacked me, and I fenced with them like a frantic fury till I got inside one fellows lance and cut him half through the body. He fell: and the other over rushed himself in a charge and let me parry his thrust. Next second I had cut his throat with a back-handed slash, and presently I was up in his saddle, and scurrying back for dear life.'

After the battle of Inkerman he was with a detachment fetching in the casualties when he came upon a wounded Russian corporal who pretended he was unable to walk. Private Brown gave him a drink of water, and as he turned away to fetch an ambulance, the enemy soldier shot at him and the bullet went within an inch of his ear. Private Brown made him walk into the lines at the point of his sabre. 'I escaped without a wound, and with nothing worse than a dose of rheumatism, which sticks to me worse than a brother whenever the weather changes.'

He returned to Portsmouth on the *Calcutta*, receiving the Crimea Medal with *Alma, Balaclava, Inkerman* and *Sebastopol* clasps, and the Turkish Medal. He was in possession of four Good Conduct badges. He was promoted corporal on 13 December 1860, and sergeant on 1 June 1863. As a result of his service in the Crimea he suffered badly with rheumatism, and after receiving a severe rupture he discharged at Dublin on 2 June 1864, with a pension of fifteen pence a day.

His intended place of residence was Trafalgar Square in York, where he became a horse dealer, but he had some bad luck and lost all his savings. In his account he stated: 'Then I took a place as a riding master at a school in Fallowfield, Manchester, where Owens College now stands. I lost that situation when the ground was taken over and got a job as yardman at Hall & Rogers sanitary tube works, which stood on the site of St James's Hall. I was with that firm for fifteen years and a half, and got notice to leave when they dissolved the partnership.

Since then I have done little or nothing. I put in a few weeks lately at Lewis's, in Market Street, where I stood outside in my uniform and wearing my medals, giving bills away with electric lights on my shoulders and a ticket on my breast saying who and what I was. Not very pleasant for an old soldier with a spark of pride in his bosom; but a man must eat and have a roof to cover him, and anyhow it was honest work and worth a pound a week while it lasted. I left through slackness'.

In 1902 Private Pennington stated of Sergeant Brown: 'For twelve years subsequent to his retirement from the service he worked (often knee deep in water) at a canal side in Manchester, but when age and rheumatism rendered him incapable, he was compelled to go to the workhouse'.

He attended the first Balaclava banquet in 1875, was a member of the Balaclava Commemoration Society, 1879, and he signed the Loyal Address in 1887. He attended a benefit concert at the Free Trade Hall in Manchester, on 21 May 1890. He was living in lodgings at 87 Renshaw Street, Hulme, but only three months after the Manchester benefit he was admitted to the Union Workhouse at Withington, having been in an undernourished state, unable to look after himself. He was found with a sovereign in his pocket, which suggests his condition was caused by neglect; however, suffering from severe rheumatism, and working outdoors would have seriously affected his health. He died in the Withington Workhouse, on 20 August 1890, aged sixty-five, and he was buried in a subscription grave at Philips Park Cemetery, Manchester.

WILLIAM BUTLER
17TH LANCERS

William Butler was born at Ormskirk, Lancashire, in 1825, and was brought up in Preston. When his father died his uncle taught him the trade of shoemaking and he earned his living at this in Manchester, before moving to Yorkshire. After being impressed by stories told him by a young Lancer in Sheffield, he decided to enlist, and joined the 17th Lancers at Nottingham in April 1846.

Two months later Private Butler went with the regiment to Dundalk in Ireland, which at the time was suffering from the terrible potato famine. He was orderly to the Earl of Clarendon at Dublin, before returning to his regiment. In an account he published in 1890 he stated: 'They were hard times for us in 1848, during Smith O'Brien's time; we had to do duty every other night. I was one of the escort which took him from the Four Courts, after he was sentenced to be hung, drawn and quartered, to Harold's Cross Gaol. I was hit with a stone on my head, and bear the mark of the blow to this day.'

Private Butler was on escort duty, riding close to the royal coach, when Queen Victoria and Prince Albert, and other members of the Royal Family visited Dublin. On returning to England he was on parade at the Great Exhibition in Hyde Park in 1851, and in the following year he was present at the funeral of the Duke of Wellington. He was on despatch duty in Kensington when the Crimean War broke out and orders to mobilise were received.

He embarked on *The Pride of the Ocean* at Portsmouth in April 1854 to sail to Turkey, and was devastated when his favourite horse was one of fifteen swept overboard as the ship ship rolled badly in rough seas in the Bay of Biscay.

He was present at the battle of the Alma, and at Inkerman, and he took part in the Light Brigade action at Balaclava. His account states: 'My blood was up, and I began to wish to get near to the enemy. Shot and shell were coming in all directions. What few reached the guns - and I amongst them cut away like madmen and succeeded in taking and spiking them. Coming back I was attacked by two

Cossacks. I engaged the one on my right, and dispatched him at the time the other made a cut at me which just caught my nose, chin, and bridle hand; but he never cut another, for I left him on the ground. Going a little further my horse was shot beneath me and I lay weltering in blood and swooned. I should think I must have lain there two or three hours before I came to. I did not know where I was until a French sentry challenged me, and I was taken to a French doctor, who dressed my wounds. I did not get back to my own lines until next day.

We were ordered from the front in December 1854, for both men and horses were starving. The horses were actually eating each other, whilst the men were frost-bitten. The food comprised green berries of coffee, and there was no fire to cook anything. I did not care if I lived or not. I have often had to be dug up with a spade, my hair being frozen to the tent. I shall never forget Christmas Day, 1854. I was nearly dead with hunger and filth, and I wished to die, but my time had not come.'

After narrowly escaping serious injury in a stable fire in Turkey, he returned home, where he was one of three Lancers who represented the Regiment at an inspection by Queen Victoria in Portsmouth. For his service in the East he received the Crimea Medal with *Alma, Balaclava, Inkerman* and *Sebastopol* clasps, and the Turkish Medal.

In May 1857, religious fanaticism and opposition to British rule and modernisation caused unrest among the soldiers of the Bengal Army in the north of India, which flared-up into widespread rebellion, and Sergeant Butler sailed to India on the *Great Britain* for service under Hugh Rose in the advance to suppress the Indian Mutiny. For his service he received the Indian Mutiny Medal with *Central India* clasp.

He was taking his discharge in 1863, when the Adjutant of the 18th (Royal Irish) Regiment persuaded him to transfer, and he was appointed Master Boot Maker and sergeant. He took his final discharge at Aldershot in October 1867, with a pension of fifteen and a half pence a day, and he received a Long Service, Good Conduct Medal. In his account he states: 'I went to London, started business, and was doing very well until I had some little trouble about property and I lost the day. That started my bad luck. I had a deal of sickness in my family, and doctors bills pulled me down. I had to leave London for my health, and came to Preston, where I got a little shoemaking (at Black Horse Yard), and lived there for five years. The ill health of my wife caused me to leave Preston, and I came to live at South Shore, Blackpool.'

He attended the first Balaclava reunion banquet, was a member of the Balaclava Commemoration Society, and he signed the Loyal Address. He also attended the Manchester benefit in 1890.

Sergeant Butler died on 13 February 1901, aged seventy-five, and he was buried in Layton Cemetery, Blackpool. A contemporary report stated: 'The late Sergeant William Butler, who died at Preston on Wednesday, was well-known at Blackpool, where he lived for many years. His figure, which sported four hard-won medals, was a very conspicuous one there.'

JOHN CHADWICK
17TH LANCERS

John Chadwick was born in 1817, of Irish descent. He enlisted into the 17th Lancers, being promoted Cornet on 27 February 1852, and Lieutenant on 25 October 1854.

During the Light Brigade action at Balaclava he reached the Russian battery, but his already half-starved horse had been wounded and weakened from loss of blood, and he could not get it to move any further. He tried to defend himself against Cossacks, but a lance point in his neck knocked him from his mount and rendered him helpless. He thus became one of only two officers to be taken prisoner, the other being Cornet Clowes, and he was released with all the surviving Allied prisoners a year later. For his service in the East he received the Crimea Medal with *Alma, Balaclava* and *Sebastopol* clasps. He exchanged into the 15th Hussars on half-pay, 29 April 1856, where he became a honorary Captain in 1858. He was appointed Adjutant and Quartermaster at the Royal Hospital, Kilmainham, Dublin. He had married Jane Maitland at Stirling, and when she died in Dublin in 1867, and as he himself was in failing health, he decided to retire in December of that year. In 1864 during a lawsuit concerning whether Lord Cardigan had reached the Russian battery at Balaclava, Captain Chadwick wrote a letter to support a statement made in court by Patrick Rafferty, 17th Lancers, which confirmed that Lord Cardigan had reached the Russian guns.

He retired to Liverpool, where he lived at 25 Hurst Street, Liverpool 1. He died at the Southern Hospital, Greenlands Street, Liverpool, on 25 March 1869, aged fifty-one. Cause of death was recorded as being from cirrhosis ascites (certified). He was buried in Anfield Cemetery, Liverpool.

Photographs of a group of 17th Lancers in dress uniform taken soon after their return from the Crimea, and a party of 17th Lancers veterans at a Balaclava reunion.

DANIEL DEERING
4TH LIGHT DRAGOONS

Daniel Deering was born in Dublin in 1826, and enlisted into the 4th Light Dragoons on 27 November 1846. He served in the Crimea, taking part in the Light Brigade action at Balaclava, and received the Crimea Medal with *Alma, Balaclava, Inkerman* and *Sebastopol* clasps, and the Turkish Medal.

In 1863 he was serving as a private in B Troop, 4th Hussars, at Newbridge in Ireland, when he was asked to submit evidence concerning the lawsuit brought by Lord Cardigan against Lord Calthorpe, who had made disparaging remarks about his conduct during the Charge. Trooper Deering stated: "When we were charging up to the battery and within three hundred yards of it, we met Lord Cardigan alone, returning to the rear on a chestnut horse. He was cantering back and was to the left of the 4th Light Dragoons. I know Lord Cardigan well and I am quite certain it was him. I was retiring. He rode up to us and said: 'This has been a great blunder, but don't blame me for it".

On his discharge from the army he settled in Nottingham, where he became a caretaker at a school, living in a room which was part of the school building, at 36 Virginia Street, in the parish of St Mary's, Byron. His wife, Hannah, who came from Cromford in Derbyshire, was fourteen years younger and worked at the local laundry. By 1881 they lived at 7 Hudson Street, Bluebell Hill, Manvers, and Daniel was also working at the laundry.

He attended the first Balaclava Reunion Banquet in 1875, was a member of the Balaclava Commemoration Society, 1879, and he signed the Loyal Address in 1887. He attended three annual dinners in 1893, 1895 and 1897. He was a member of the Nottingham Crimean and Indian Mutiny Veterans' Association, and at least three fellow Cavalrymen, Sergeant-Major Thomas Morley, Trooper Matthew Holland and Sergeant-Major George Watson were also members. He was a pensioner of the TH Roberts Fund.

He was described as an army pensioner living at 10 Harvey Terrace, St Anne's, Manvers, when he died on 30 May 1904, aged seventy-eight; as plans for celebrating the fiftieth anniversary of the Charge were being made. His wife Hannah survived him.

Thomas Morley and Matthew Holland attended the funeral at St Barnabas's Cathedral, and Daniel was buried in the Roman Catholic section of Nottingham General Cemetery, with military honours provided by a detachment of the Robin Hood Rifles. The only relatives who followed were Mrs and Miss Heard.

Local newspapers reported that he was one of three local old veterans who had died within two days of each other. Ex-Colour-Sergeant Thomas Francis, and Thomas Hames, 95th (Derbyshire) Regiment, aged eighty-two, who was placed in the same grave as Trooper Deering.

JAMES DONOGHUE
8TH HUSSARS

James Donoghue was born into a military family, on 25 October 1829, and followed his grandfather and father into the Army when, at the age of fourteen, he joined the 8th Hussars. He was five feet seven inches tall, with a fresh complexion, hazel eyes and brown hair.

He embarked for the Crimea on the *Mendora*, on 27 April 1854, being appointed field trumpeter to Colonel Shewell. He was present at the battle of the Alma, and he was celebrating his birthday when he took part in the Light Brigade action at Balaclava, where his horse was shot from under him. He reverted to private on 12 April 1855, and was later promoted to corporal. For his service in the East he was awarded the Crimea Medal with *Alma, Balaclava, Inkerman* and *Sebastopol* clasps, the Turkish Medal, and he was one of only four soldiers in the 8th Hussars to be awarded a French War Medal.

On 8 October 1857 he embarked on the Great Britain to sail to Bombay for active service in the Indian Mutiny, under Sir Hugh Rose, for which he received the Indian Mutiny Medal with *Central India* clasp. He was invalided out of the Army soon after returning from India, his health having been damaged by sunstroke and rheumatic fever. He had never been entered in the defaulters book, and he was awarded a pension of eight pence a day.

On 2 June 1863 he filed an affidavit in the Cardigan lawsuit. At the time he was a Bandmaster with the 1st (Exeter and S[c] Devon) Volunteer Rifle Regiment, an[d] was living in Black Boy Road, Exeter. later became attached to the Staffords[] Regiment, and then the South Lancas[] Regiment, which took him to Warringto[n] Cheshire (which was then in Lancashi[] where he made his home in the villag[e] Penketh.

In 1875 it was reported in the local p[] that he could not afford the fare to trave[] London for the first Balaclava reunion b[] quet. However, he was a member of Balaclava Commemoration Society, and attended a benefit show performed at Free Trade Hall in Manchester on 21 [] 1890, to raise funds for the survivors of Light Brigade who were living in the n[] of England. The concert raised nearly t[] hundred pounds.

James Donoghue was described as respected member of the community', [] was known to give recitations of his lif[e] the Army which were said to be 'interest[] and popular.' He died at Penke[] Warrington, on 17 November 1894, a[g] sixty-five. He was buried in St Mar[] Churchyard, Penketh; his grave being p[] for by friends and admirers. An app[] fund was set up to help his wid[c] Elizabeth, who died in 1909 and was bur[] with him. His grave was rediscovered b[] youth development worker in the 1980[] and it was renovated. A wreath was laid the grave during the 1998 remembran[] parade, and a bugler played the *Last Pos[]*

JOHN DOYLE
8TH HUSSARS

John Doyle was born in Ireland in 1830, where he joined the 8th Hussars at Newbridge Depot, on 21 February 1850. His brother was serving with the 73rd Highlanders (Black Watch), and John made a personal request to the Duke of Cambridge for him to be transferred to the 8th Hussars. Unfortunately, before the transfer papers arrived he was ordered to South Africa on the troopship *Birkenhead*, and perished when the ship was wrecked in February 1852.

Private Doyle was on Horse Guards duty at the Great Exhibition in 1851, and in the following year he was present at the funeral of the Duke of Wellington. He also formed part of an escort for Queen Victoria on several occasions. The regiment was stationed at Exeter when orders were received for active service in the East, and they embarked on the troopship *Willie Canada* at Devonport, for what proved to be a perilous journey. 'We were a long time knocking about in the Bay of Biscay, and we all expected to go down; we threw some horses overboard to lighten the ship, and afterwards arrived safely in Constantinople.' John was with the unit of 8th Hussars which took part in the notorious 'Sore Back' reconnaissance with Lord Cardigan.

He kept a diary about his experiences in the Army, and in 1877 he published a booklet in Manchester, in which he states that during the Light Brigade action at Balaclava: 'We charged under a most terrific fire from cannon and musketry; on our right were three tiers of guns and infantry as thick as they could be placed; and on our right was one tier of guns and infantry in masses; so that the shot and shell, grape, canister and musketry came upon us like hail. My horse, *(Hickabod)*, got a bullet through the nose, which caused him to lose a great deal of blood, and every time he gave his head a chuck the blood spurted over me. That night when I opened my cloak I found twenty-seven bullets in it. There were five buttons blown off my dress jacket; the slings of my sabretache were cut off, but my sword belts were not touched. I also had the right heel and spur blown off my boot. It was a long and terrible charge.

Going into the Charge I had the first finger of the bridle hand split in five places and a piece cut out of my thumb, and on coming out I got a fair point of a lance in the forehead, but I did not know there was a hole in it for a week or ten days afterwards... Being young, supple, and like an eel in the saddle, I could turn and twist as quickly as lightening. I must have wounded many of them, as I did nothing but parry their points and return my own as quickly as I could.

There was an officer who dashed into the centre of us... I had pointed him with a 'right-rear point,' and just as the Russian retreat sounded I saw the same officer endeavouring to get in front of me; and when he heard the sound he turned short to the left, and met me right hand to right hand, and made a terrible point at me; but I had my eyes on him, for I knew I had pointed him in rear of the guns, and he would have me if he could, but, thank God, I was too quick for him! I parried off his point, and with a return point drove my sword through his mouth. I still kept on the swing, and saw nothing more of him.

Soon afterwards I came in contact with Colonel Shewell, who was in the ploughed ground. Knowing the ground well, as I used to pass over it nearly every day, and being on a pathway, I shouted to get back on my track, or he would never get across. He took my advice, inclined to his right, and got on my track.

When I got back no one knew me, for I was covered with blood from my head to my feet. My comrades knew the horse, but did not know who I was. Colonel Shewell called out to know who I was, then told me to take my horse to the commissary officer and shoot him! He thought he was done for. I would have soon have lost my own life, as to have shot my horse, who had so gallantly carried me through the vicissitudes of that eventful but glorious day. The wound healed rapidly, and by the battle of Inkerman my horse was as well as ever.'

After suffering the hardships of the harsh Crimean winter, during which he had to: 'give up and go into hospital for want of clothes', Private Doyle embarked for England on 24 April 1856, where he was inspected by Queen Victoria at a parade in Portsmouth. For his service in the East he received the Crimea Medal with *Alma*, *Balaclava*, *Inkerman* and *Sebastopol* clasps, and the Turkish Medal.

On 8 October 1857 he embarked from Cork on the *Great Britain* for service in the Indian Mutiny. 'We disembarked at Bombay on 18 December, and as soon as we landed there were two of the sepoy rebel chiefs blown from the guns.

We then marched to Kotah, after the siege of that place. At last we got the orders to advance, and a terrible affair it was. We fought for about twenty miles after the rebels and only ceased the pursuit when night came on. We had to march back over the same ground we had fought over during the day, and had to swim the river back. Next day we again took to the field, and were twelve months engaged, not many days passing without a battle.' For his service he received the Indian Mutiny Medal with *Central India* clasp.

On his return home he was posted to various stations throughout Britain. He discharged in September 1873, after twenty-two years service. 'Afterwards we went to Curragh Camp, and then to Longford, where I retired after so many hair-breadth escapes, upon an acknowledgement of one shilling and one penny a day.'

He became Sergeant, Drill Instructor, and by 1876 he was living in Ordsall, Salford, with his wife, Mary, and three children. Firstly at 12 Darley Street, then 44 Ellesmere Street. In 1886 he moved to 27 Platt Street, Moss Side, Manchester. He eventually moved to Liverpool, where he died in the Royal Infirmary in August 1892. He was buried in the Roman Catholic section of Anfield Cemetery, Liverpool, on 16 August 1892.

JOHN BURGHERSH FORBES
4TH *LIGHT DRAGOONS*

John Forbes was born at Dull, near Perth, Scotland, in 1821. He was employed as a clerk prior to enlisting into the 9th Lancers at Maidstone on 10 October 1845, being described as aged twenty-four, five feet eight inches tall, with blue eyes, brown hair and a dark complexion. He was promoted corporal only a month later, on 12 November, being appointed sergeant on 10 March 1847. He transferred to the 4th Light Dragoons as sergeant on 1 July 1847, and reverted to private 'at his own request' on 13 December 1850.

He saw service in the Crimea, and took part in the Light Brigade action at Balaclava. He had two horses shot under him and returned to the British lines on a third, although he was without serious injury, and he was promoted to corporal later that day. He was promoted sergeant on 26 February 1855, 'by authority of Lt-General George Scovell, 4th Light Dragoons, dated 13 December 1854.' This promotion may have been because of his conduct with the Light Brigade at Balaclava, as it was not usual procedure for a promotion to be recorded accompanied by any particular authority. he was appointed Troop Sergeant-Major on 22 July 1855. For his services in the East he received the Crimea Medal with *Alma, Balaclava, Inkerman* and *Sebastopol* clasps, and the Turkish Medal.

He was awarded a Long Service, Good Conduct Medal on 20 December 1866, and he had five Good Conduct badges. He discharged from Canterbury on 3 November

1869, 'Free, after twenty-four years service', being granted a pension of two shillings a day.

He lived at the Riding School, Bath Road, Newcastle-upon-Tyne, taking an appointment as staff sergeant with the Northumberland Hussars Yeomanry Cavalry, on 3 November 1869. He discharged from the Northumberland Hussars on 30 October 1882 - 'on account of age' - which was sixty years. His conduct had been 'highly satisfactory', his pension was increased, and he had a total military service of over thirty-seven years.

He attended the Balaclava banquet in 1875, was a member of the Balaclava Commemoration Society, and he signed the Loyal Address in 1887. He attended the annual dinners in 1890 and 1893.

The first Balaclava banquet held at the Alexandra Palace in 1875.

He became ill in the Spring of 1895, and in August he missed his duty training with the Northumberland Fusiliers for the first time in thirty years; although he watched the manouvres from a closed carriage. John Forbes died on 31 August 1895, aged seventy-six, at his home in Northumberland Road, Newcastle. He left five sons and a daughter.

He was buried in St Andrews Cemetery, Newcastle, with military honours provided by the Northumberland Fusiliers. His sword, busby and medals had been placed on the coffin, and his funeral was attended by Private Robert Nichol. On Armistice Day 1954, to commemorate the centenary of the battle of Balaclava, a wreath was placed at the grave.

JAMES GLANISTER
11TH HUSSARS

James Glanister was born at Finedon, near Wellingborough, Northamptonshire, in 1834, the younger brother of George Glanister. He had worked as a labourer prior to enlisting into the 5th Dragoon Guards (Princess Charlotte of Wales's), at Liverpool on 6 June 1852. He was aged eighteen years three months, was five feet seven inches tall, with a fresh complexion, grey eyes and light brown hair. His brother had served with the 11th Hussars since 1849, so he transferred into that regiment on 31 October 1852, and they both went to the Crimea from the Newbridge depot on 24 July 1854.

He took part in the Light Brigade action at Balaclava. Robert Martin, 11th Hussars, stated: 'Just at that moment my right arm was shattered to pieces. I gathered it up as well as I could and laid it across my knees. While fighting in the midst of the guns Glanister unfortunately broke his sword off short at the hilt by striking a Russian on the top of his helmet. The order to retire was given by Lord George Paget, and on turning I saw a Cossack close to us. He immediately levelled his pistol and fired. The bullet whizzed by my face and struck Glanister, shattering his lower jaw and causing him to fall forward on his cloak, which was rolled up in front of him. The Cossack bolted at once, and I had the presence of mind to place the reins of my horse in my mouth, at the same time seizing those of Glanister's horse and turning it into the ranks. By this means, no doubt, his life was saved.'

RSM Loy Smith, 11th Hussars, stated: 'As we neared the battery, a square of infantry that had been placed a little in advance of the guns, gave us a volley in flank. The very air hissed as the shower of bullets passed through us; many men were now killed or wounded. Private Glanister had his lower jaw shattered by a bullet entering on the right side...'

Private Glanister was seriously wounded, and was invalided from Scutari to England on 29 October 1854. He was entitled to the Crimea Medal with *Alma, Balaclava* and *Sebastopol* clasps, and both he and Private Martin were awarded the Distinguished Conduct Medal. They were among many Crimean casualties who were presented before Queen Victoria in the Mess Room at Brompton Barracks, on 3 March 1855. He was discharged from Chatham Invalid Depot on 10 July 1855, 'Unfit for further service by fracture of the lower jaw by a pistol shot (on the right side). Articulation and motion of the lower jaw is impaired'.

James Glanister attended the first Balaclava Banquet in 1875, he was a member of the Balaclava Commemoration Society, 1879. He attended the Manchester benefit in 1890, and he was at the Annual Dinners in 1893 and 1895. He was invited to the Jubilee Celebrations in Fleet Street in 1897.

He died at his residence, 3 Apple Terrace, Edge Hill, Liverpool, on 24 March 1901, aged sixty-eight. He was buried in West Derby Cemetery, Liverpool.

EDWARD HINDLEY
13TH LIGHT DRAGOONS

Edward Hindley was born at Liverpool in 1831, and enlisted into the 13th Light Dragoons in 1853. Private Hindley was present at the battle of the Alma, and at Inkerman, and he took part in the Light Brigade action at Balaclava. He was later promoted to Sergeant. For his service in the East he received the Crimea Medal with *Alma, Balaclava, Inkerman* and *Sebastopol* clasps, and the Turkish Medal.

In 1857 he went to India for service in the Mutiny, for which he received the Indian Mutiny Medal with *Lucknow* clasp.

On his discharge he lived with his wife, Emma, who was a dressmaker, at 17 Granby Street, Princess Park, Liverpool 8, before moving to 2 Woodcroft Road, Wavertree, Liverpool 15.

He was a member of the Balaclava Commemoration Society, 1879, and he attended a number of Annual Dinners, including the 1895 dinner in Birmingham, his last visit being in 1910.

He died at his home on 21 November 1911, aged eighty, and he was buried with military honours in Toxteth Park Cemetery, Smithdown Road, Liverpool, four days later. There is no memorial stone.

He had received help from the T H Roberts Fund, which paid his funeral expenses and supported his widow. Mr Roberts also sent a wreath. Edward Hindley's Medals were left to Mr Roberts and were still with his family until February 1998, when they were sold at auction for over twelve thousand pounds.

The two surviving Liverpool veterans, Edward Hindley (back row, third from right) and William Sewell (middle row, third from left) at the 1906 Balaclava reunion.

JOHN HOGAN
8TH *HUSSARS*

John Hogan was born in Tipperary, Ireland in November 1828, and enlisted into the 8th Hussars at Dublin on 13 February 1847, at the age of nineteen. He was five feet nine inches tall, with a fresh complexion, hazel eyes and light-brown hair.

The regiment were stationed at Brighton when they received orders for active service in the East, and on 25 April 1854, they embarked on the heavy transport *Shooting Star*. Hogan took part in the Light Brigade action at Balaclava, afterwards stating that he 'brought his horse out of the engagement without a scratch.' For his service he received the Crimea Medal with *Balaclava*, *Inkerman* and *Sebastopol* clasps and the Turkish Medal.

On 8 October 1857 he embarked from Cork on the *Great Britain* and sailed for a second posting of active service, this time to northern India where the Indian Mutiny was raging. He took part in all the major engagements in Central India, including the charge at Gwalior, and had the second finger of his sword hand shot away. He remained in India for six years, and for his service he received the Indian Mutiny Medal with *Central India* clasp.

He returned to Portsmouth with the regiment, and after a few months of Home service he discharged from the army at Edinburgh on 17 December 1868, just a month short of his forty-first birthday. He was in possession of two good conduct badges.

He went to live with friends in Leeds, where he remained for some time before moving to The Shambles in York, where he worked as an out-porter, and became: 'well-known in York as a Balaclava hero.'

He attended the first Balaclava Reunion Banquet in 1875, was a member of the Balaclava Commemoration Society, and he signed the Loyal Address in 1887. He attended the Reunion Dinner at St James's Restaurant, London, in 1893.

John Hogan died at 3 Lord's Yard, The Shambles, York, on 24 June 1900, in his seventy-second year. Local newspapers reported that: 'Hogan was a fine old soldier, and his record should have assured him at least comfort in his old age and decent interment.' However, an appeal for public funds was needed to pay his funeral expenses and meet his last wish to keep him 'off the parish.' He was buried in York Cemetery (public grave 12321).

MATTHEW HOLLAND
11TH HUSSARS

Matthew Holland was born on 23 June 1833, at Pimlico, London, and was christened at St Anne's Church, Soho, Westminster, on 18 August that year. His parents, John and Elizabeth (formerly Heartis), had married in the same church on 28 August 1831. The family moved to Nottingham when Matthew was about six years old.

He enlisted into the 11th Hussars at Westminster, London, on 18 May 1852, and two years later sailed for active service in the East, where he took part in the Light Brigade action at Balaclava. He was at Scutari Hospital in the Spring of 1855, where he volunteered to be cook and odd-job man for Florence Nightingale, of whom he spoke highly. The rigours of being on constant alert, with a lack of provisions wore the men down and in December 1856 he was court martialled for being found asleep at his post. He was sentenced to eighty-four days imprisonment with hard labour. For his service he received the Crimea Medal with *Alma, Balaclava, Inkerman* and *Sebastopol* clasps and the Turkish Medal.

On his return to England he requested to transfer to the 8th Hussars for active service in the Sepoy Rebellion, landing in India on 19 December 1857. He served with the Central India Field Force under Hugh Rose, taking part in the actions at Kotah on 30 March and the charge at Gwalior on 17 June, for which the regiment gained four Victoria Crosses. For his service he received the Indian Mutiny Medal with *Central India* clasp. He discharged at York on 17 August 1864, having twice seen major active service during his twelve years in the cavalry.

He made his living as a journeyman painter and in the September quarter of 1867, he married Hannah (formerly Beckworth). She was a Nottingham girl who had an eight year old son named John, born when she was sixteen. They made their home at 153 Corby Street, Brightside, Sheffield. By 1881 they had returned to Nottingham, and lived at 12 Platt Street, St Mary's, and by 1891 they had moved to nearby 6 Snow Hill, where Hannah's sister, Mary, and their grandson, Matthew, also came to live.

Trooper Holland served with the pioneers of the Robin Hood Rifles, always on parade in any weather as a good example to young men. He attended the first Balaclava reunion banquet in 1875, was a member of the Balaclava Commemoration Society, and he signed the Loyal Address. He attended several annual reunion dinners, and he was an active member of the Crimean and Indian Mutiny Veterans' Association.

Matthew Holland died on 14 December 1912, aged seventy-nine, at 15 Virginia Street, Byron, Nottingham, leaving a widow. He was buried in the Veterans' Ground of Nottingham General Cemetery with military honours provided by several units including the 11th Hussars.

JOHN HOWES
4TH *LIGHT DRAGOONS*

John Howes was born at Wymondham near Norwich in 1828. He enlisted into the 4th Light Dragoons on 16 November 1846, and was later promoted sergeant. He sailed to the East with the regiment, and was one of the most heavily engaged cavalrymen during the Light Brigade action at Balaclava. He assisted one of his officers, Cornet Hunt, in an effort to capture a Russian cannon. However, they did not succeed because the horses had become too frenzied and could not be got under control. He received a sword-cut to the side of his head during an engagement with an enemy Hussar, and he is believed to have been the last man to get back to the British lines. A Birmingham newspaper reported that he had stated: 'It was no fault on my part,' he has humorously remarked, 'it was all owing to a brute of a horse I had - not my own.' For his service he received the Crimea Medal with *Alma, Balaclava, Inkerman* and *Sebastopol* clasps, and the Turkish Medal. He discharged from the army as Troop Sergeant-Major in 1860.

He settled in Birmingham where he lived for most of the time at 23 Spring Road, Edgbaston. Described as being: 'Tall, slightly-built and erect. Looking several years younger than his age.' He became a highly-respected member of the community, showing much concern for the welfare of ex-servicemen in Birmingham. With Sergeant John Parkinson, he helped to form the Birmingham Military Veterans' Association, to assist local survivors of the Crimean War and Indian Mutiny campaigns and to which he became honorary treasurer, organising the reunion dinners held just before Christmas each year. In December 1894 they held their first reunion dinner at the Old Royal Hotel, Temple Row, Birmingham, which was attended by Lord Roberts VC. This was a great success, so the Balaclava Commemoration Society, of which he was a member, agreed to hold their 1895 reunion at the same venue, and Sergeant Howes took a leading part in its organisation. He had signed the Loyal Address in 1887, and attended the 1892 Balaclava Reunion Banquet.

His obituary states: 'Sergeant Howes formed one of the Guard of Honour at Birmingham Town Hall to Mr Joseph Chamberlain, on the occasion of the great banquet in commemoration of the right honourable gentleman's mission to South Africa. On the occasion Mr Chamberlain shook hands with the sergeant-major (who looked very smart in the full uniform of his regiment) and expressed pleasure that, in his advanced years, he was enjoying excellent health.' He was described as: 'A valuable and devoted colleague, and a sincere and warmhearted friend.'

On leaving the Old Royal Hotel after the BMVA annual dinner on 18 December 1902 he is believed to have caught a cold. Within days this had developed into pneumonia and he died at his home on 25 December 1902, aged seventy-four. He was buried with military honours at Lodge Hill Cemetery, Selly Oak, Birmingham.

EDWIN HUGHES
13TH LIGHT DRAGOONS

Edwin Hughes was born in Mount Street, Wrexham, on 12 December 1830, the son of a tinplate worker. He is known to have had a sister named Susan. He worked as a shoemaker prior to his enlistment into the 13th Light Dragoons on 28 October 1852, and he joined the regiment at Hounslow on 6 May 1853. He was stationed at Great Brook Street Barracks, Birmingham, when orders were received for active service in the East, and he sailed from Portsmouth with the regiment.

He took part in the Light Brigade action at Balaclava, and left three accounts of his experiences that day: *Birmingham, 1904*: 'When we started twenty cannon as well as musketry blazed at us. Never was there such a death-dealing business, and half the saddles were empty in no time. Then, before guns crossing the valley could be charged for another round, we were engaged dispatching the gunners. It was a terrible hand-to-hand slaughter. My horse was shot and I fell partly under the plunging animal, my leg was lacerated and crushed and I got a slight sword wound in the face, but I managed to get to the British lines, and was soon guarding Russian prisoners taken earlier in the day.'

Answers Magazine, 1912: 'I rode fifth file, front rank, right of first line. On coming within range of the guns, the horse I rode was shot, and fell with me underneath, and for a considerable time I was unable to move, as my left leg was fast. During this time the second and third line passed over

me, but I escaped being trodden on. I got free at last, and made the best of my way back. I was damaged about the face and left leg, but not seriously.'

Blackpool, 1921: 'I was on duty that day from four o'clock in the morning until after the Charge in the afternoon. We rode out at the command straight for the Russian lines. Before we reached them my horse was shot, and in falling on its side I got partially pinned underneath, injuring my leg. I was assisted away, and was then placed in charge of some Russians for the rest of the day and the following night.'

'You never think of honours or glory at the time, but I am proud now that I was in the

Charge. There was death all around us, but it was a glorious affair, and I have never regretted that I was there.'

He came to be known as 'Balaclava Ned' on his return to Britain, before retiring from the Army as Squadron Sergeant-Major in 1873. He had served for twenty-one years, and was presented with a marble clock by the NCOs of the regiment. He settled in Birmingham with his wife, and served as Instructor to the Worcestershire Yeomanry for twelve years from 1874 to 1886. They had four children, Theophilus, Blanche, Mary and Horace, who was known as Ernest.

He was a member of the Balaclava Commemoration Society, 1879, and he attended several Annual Dinners, including the one held at the Old Royal Hotel, Temple Row, Birmingham in 1895, and the last one in 1913.

In 1905 he moved to Blackpool to live with his unmarried daughter, Mary, at 64 Egerton Road, North Shore. On his ninety-first birthday in 1921 he was interviewed for the local newspaper and was described as having 'a voice as bell-clear as when he drilled recruits in the Army', and he was said to be 'hale and hearty, and wonderfully erect and active. However, he was rather deaf.' He received financial help from the TH Roberts Fund, and in 1918 he was granted a pension from the Royal Patriotic Fund. He also received a special pension granted by the War Office for the last two years of his life.

Edwin Hughes, the last survivor of the Light Brigade action at Balaclava, died peacefully at his home on 18 May 1927, aged ninety-six. He was buried in Layton Cemetery, Blackpool, with military honours provided by several Regiments, including the 13th Light Dragoons. In 1992 a commemorative plaque was place at the house where he was born, and on 2 March 2005, his medals were bought back into the family from an auction in London for sixteen thousand pounds.

The Crimea Medal (with Alma, Balaclava, Inkerman and Sebastopol clasps), a Long Service Good Conduct Medal and the Turkish Medal, which was given by the Sultan of Turkey to all men who had served in the Crimea.

THOMAS EVERARD-HUTTON
4TH *LIGHT DRAGOONS*

Thomas Hutton was born at Beverley in the East Riding of Yorkshire, on 13 April 1821, the son of Henry Hutton, Barrister-at-Law of Lincoln. He entered the 15th Foot (East Yorkshire Regiment), as Ensign, on 21 June 1839, being promoted Lieutenant on 6 May 1842. He exchanged into the 4th Light Dragoons on 10 September 1847, being appointed Captain on 23 April 1852. He sailed for active service in the East on the *Simla*, disembarking on 4 August 1854. He was present at the battle of the Alma, and took part in the Light Brigade action at Balaclava.

The Regimental History states: 'Hutton was shot through the right thigh as he rode up the valley, and reported the wound to Captain Low, his squadron leader. 'If you can sit on your horse,' replied Low, 'you had better come on with us; there's no use going back now, you'll only be killed.' Accordingly Hutton rode on, fought through the guns and returned with the regiment. As they rode back up the valley Hutton was shot in the other thigh but remained on his horse. Colonel Paget overtook him, saw that he was hurt and faint, and passed him his rum flask. Hutton thanked him and said, 'I have been wounded, Colonel. Would you have any objection to my going to the doctor when I get in?'

His horse had eleven wounds and had to be destroyed. He was sent to Scutari on the *Australia*, and after making a good recovery he sailed to Malta and was invalided home to England on 21 March 1855.

For his service he was awarded the Crimea Medal with *Alma*, *Balaclava* and *Sebastopol* clasps, and the Turkish Medal. The Crimea Medal was presented to him by Queen Victoria at Horse Guards Parade on 18 May 1855. He was appointed Brevet-Major on 6 June 1856. He retired by sale of commission on 10 October 1857.

On 14 August 1856, he married Maria Georgina, only child of Edward Everard, of Middleton Hall, King's Lynn, and in 1864 he assumed the surname Everard-Hutton. He resided at Middleton Hall, and then at St Asaph, Denbighshire, north Wales. He spent the last years of his life living in a magnificent house at 7 The Circus, Bath.

A memorial plaque dedicated to Major Hutton at Bath Abbey.

Major Hutton died on 10 June 1896, aged seventy-five, leaving a widow and four daughters. He was buried with military honours at Locksbrook Cemetery, Bath. The funeral was attended by Captain Percy Shaw Smith, who took part in the Light Brigade action at Balaclava with the 13th Light Dragoons. Some of his letters written after Balaclava were published in the regimental journal in October 1933.

CHARLES MACAULEY
8TH HUSSARS

Charles Macauley was born at Rawcliffe, North Yorkshire, on 3 June 1828, the son of Surgeon Richard Macauley. He was a tailor, living at 24 St Peter's Square, Leeds, when he enlisted into the 6th Dragoon Guards, at Manchester, on 3 April 1846. He was five feet ten inches tall, with a fair complexion, grey eyes and light-brown hair. He transferred to the 8th Hussars on 1 March 1848.

On 15 May 1854, he embarked on the *Echunga* for service in the East. He arrived at Balaclava from Scutari on 20 October 1854, where he took part in the Light Brigade action. He was promoted corporal on 10 January 1855, and sergeant on 29 August 1855. For his service he received the Crimea Medal with *Alma, Balacalava, Inkerman* and *Sebastopol* clasps, the Turkish Medal, and the French Military War Medal.

Sergeant Macauley was examined by a medical board at Manchester, on 17 May 1865, and was found to have been disabled by syphilis. He was discharged as unfit for further service, at York, on 13 June 1865. His character was described as 'very good', and he was in possession of five 'good conduct' badges.

He made his home at 47, The Covered Market, Leeds. Considering that he was discharged with syphilis, it is remarkable to note that in 1875, he married the daughter of Richard Crampton of Leeds, with whom he had a son and daughter.

He attended the Balaclava Banquet in 1875, was a member of the Balaclava Commemoration Society, 1879, and he signed the Loyal Address in 1887. He attended several Balaclava Annual Dinners, his last one being in 1899.

Charles Macauley settled with his family at 12 Providence Row, Clay Pit Lane, Leeds, where he died on 5 January 1905, aged seventy-six. He was buried at Woodhouse Cemetery, Leeds, which is now a landscaped area close to Leeds University. The name of Sergeant John Macauley, 8th Hussars, appears on the Crimea Memorial at Leeds Parish Church. He died of disease at Yanzibar in 1854, and is believed to have been related to Charles.

THOMAS MORLEY
17TH LANCERS

Thomas Morley was born in the parish of St Mary's, Byron, Nottingham, on 28 March 1830, the first child of William Morley and his wife Ann (formerly Menton), who had married at St Mary's Church, Byron, on 2 November 1824. His father worked for the Inland Revenue. A brother named Samuel was born in 1831, and a sister named Sabina was born in 1832. Their father died during the September quarter of 1837, and their mother died in the following December, so Thomas was placed in the Nottingham Union Workhouse. The births of two other children were registered in St Mary's, Nottingham, to a William and Ann Morley; Lelila in 1838 and Wallace in 1839.

Thomas enlisted into the 17th Lancers on 30 June 1849, and saw active service in the East. He took part in the Light Brigade action at Balaclava, and in an account by Private James Wightman, 17th Lancers, published in 1892, he states: "(We) rode rearward, breaking through party after party of Cossacks, until we heard the familiar voice of Corporal Morley, of our regiment, a great, rough, bellowing Nottingham man. He had lost his lance hat, and his long hair was flying out in the wind as he roared, 'Coom 'ere! coom 'ere! Fall in, lads, fall in!' Well, with shouts and oaths he had collected some twenty troopers of various regiments. We fell in with the handful this man of the hour had rallied to him... A body of Russian Hussars blocked our way. Morley, roaring Nottingham oaths by way of encouragement, led us straight at them,

and we went through and out at the other side as if they had been made of tinsel paper... Not many of Corporal Morley's party got back... Morley took his discharge in 1856 because he was not awarded the Distinguished Conduct Medal, which certainly should have been given to him."

Corporal Morley took part in the battle of Inkerman, where he assisted in bringing the mortally wounded Cornet Clevland back to the British lines. He was promoted sergeant on 27 November 1854. For his service he received the Crimea Medal with *Alma, Balaclava, Inkerman and Sebastopol* clasps, and the Turkish Medal.

Sergeant Morley was upset because he was not awarded a gallantry medal, and discharged from the Army on 27 January 1857. He made many claims for the award of the Victoria Cross, until the death of his Commanding Officer, Colonel Benson, in 1892, who he blamed for his failure to get recognition for his bravery.

There was some justification for him being disgruntled. He had the support of many of his comrades who witnessed his good leadership at Balaclava, and 'Old Jack Penn', one of the men he had rallied, received the Distinguished Conduct Medal and a gold watch from the Queen! He seems to have harboured a dislike for those who gained gallantry medals, particularly Sergeant Charles Wooden, who was one of three men of the 17th Lancers to receive the Victoria Cross for action at Balaclava.

He became Drill Sergeant with the Sherwood Rangers based at Mansfield, before emigrating to the United States. He served as a Union Cavalry Officer during the American Civil War, 1861-1865. He stated that he was appointed to drill and organise a cavalry corps, and was so successful that he was given a commission. He also stated that he showed such ability in strategy, that on one occasion he broke up a large command and escaped capture, getting a thousand men away from the grip of a much superior force of the enemy. He was twice taken prisoner, and was asked by General Stonewall Jackson to take his liberty and accept a superior rank in the Confederate Army. He refused the offer and spent a year in Libby Prison. He says he was decorated for his service with the Union Army.

He returned to Britain when the conflict ended, and on 1 January 1868 took an appointment as Drill Troop Sergeant-Major with the Ayrshire Yeomanry, being promoted to Regimental Sergeant-Major on 1 June 1871. While in Scotland he married his wife, Mary, who came from Dundonald, near Ayr, and was over thirty years his junior, and they lived at Burns' Cottage in Dumfries. He resigned from the Yeomanry in June 1877.

He attended the first Balaclava Banquet, was a member of the Balaclava Commemoration Society, 1879, and he signed the Loyal Address. He is not known to have attended any of the reunion dinners.

He returned to America, where he became Quartermaster in the United States Army, gaining the rank of Captain. He later took up an appointment in the War Department in Washington, and became an American Citizen. Three sons were born to them in Washington, one of whom they named Balaclava.

He eventually returned to his native Nottingham, where he lived at 2 Manning Grove, Robin Hood. He was a member of the Nottingham Crimean and Indian Mutiny Veterans' Association, and after waiting for many years to receive a pension, it was due to the efforts of the Association that one was granted on the recommendation of Lord Tredegar in 1902. In the same year he was granted a pension from the United States Government, and he received financial help from the TH Roberts Fund. He left two accounts of his military life, in 1892 and 1899.

Captain Thomas Morley died on 14 August 1906, aged seventy-five. He was buried at Nottingham General Cemetery, with military honours provided by the 17th Lancers and the South Nottingham Hussars. His funeral was attended by Matthew Holland, who rode with the 11th Hussars at Balaclava, and Mrs Milne, said to have been the last surviving nurse who served under Florence Nightingale at Scutari.

ROBERT NICHOL
8TH HUSSARS

Robert Nichol was born on 11 September 1834, in Coventry, where his father was stationed with the 8th Hussars. His father discharged from the army two years after Robert was born, and took the family to settle in Newcastle-upon-Tyne. In 1843 Robert was sent away to attend the Royal Military Asylum adjoining the Chelsea Hospital, and had worked as a shoemaker prior to enlisting into the 8th Hussars as a very young teenager on 25 October 1848, a date which would have great significance a few years later. He was described as being five feet seven inches tall, with a fresh complexion, hazel eyes and brown hair.

He served at various Home stations, first at Newbridge, near Dublin, then Brighton, Hampton Court, Hounslow and Sheffield. The regiment was at Exeter when it received orders for active service in the East, and on 27 April 1854, embarked at Devonport on the Heavy Transport *Mendora*. Private Nichol took part in the notorious 'Bareback' reconnaissance to Silistria with Lord Cardigan, and in the Light Brigade action at Balaclava.

The Newcastle press reported: 'In the course of the return of that 'noble six hundred', the gallant Hussar saved the life of a comrade under circumstances of exceptional bravery. He stopped, when hesitation might have meant death to him, to save another fellow hero, wounded and horseless.' It is on record that John Keen, late of the 13th Light Dragoons, who was wounded in the Balaclava charge, and had his

horse killed, owed his life to the gallant assistance of Nichol, and a fellow trooper named Harrison. These two, after cutting their way through the Russian Lancers having dismounted in order to put their comrade on Nichol's horse, and convey him back to the British lines and place him under the care of a doctor.'

For his service he received the Crimea Medal with *Alma, Balaclava, Inkerman* and *Sebastopol* clasps, and the Turkish Medal.

He arrived back in England on Whit Sunday in 1856, and disembarked on the following day to be inspected by Queen Victoria. While stationed at Dundalk it became evident that the harsh conditions he had suffered in the Crimea had caused a breakdown in his constitution. He was admitted to hospital suffering with rheumatic fever, and he was discharged as unfit for further service at Dublin on 26 November 1856. His military service did not commence officially until his eighteenth birthday, and he was attributed four years service, for which he was granted a small pension of six pence a day for three years. He had a chequered military career, in that he was tried and imprisoned three times during his time in the army.

He gained employment as a landsman, and then he joined the Merchant Navy as a steward on a ship which sailed to Australia, the East Indies and Mauritius. It was reported: 'Then he returned to Newcastle and became a landsman once more. For some time he worked for the Tyne Commissioners. On one occasion he helped to paint the High-Level Bridge. He also was employed at the Forth Station, and ultimately entered the service of the Newcastle Corporation as a labourer, and for over twenty years had been intermittently in their employment, leaving them for short periods as special opportunities presented themselves. For a time he had charge of an old gentleman in Rye Hill. He returned to work under the Corporation, and for eight years was the keeper of the smallpox hospital at Byker.'

Robert attended the first Balaclava Banquet in 1875, was a member of the Balaclava Commemoration Society, and he signed the Loyal Address. He attended the annual reunion dinners in 1893 and 1895.

He lived at 13 Charlotte Street, Scotswood Road. Rheumatism and bronchitis put him in failing health for many years, and for some months prior to his death he was unable to work. Fortunately, several local people set up a benefit for him, and obtained an allowance of seven shillings a week from the Royal Patriotic Fund. He was preparing to attend the Jubilee Celebration when failing health made him bed-ridden, and he died on 18 June 1897, aged sixty-four. His coffin was carried by four Crimean veterans, as he was buried in St John's Cemetery, Elswick, Newcastle. TH Roberts sent a wreath and a donation to his widow. His Crimea Medal was sold at a Sotheby's auction on 18 February 1970.

JAMES IKIN NUNNERLEY
17TH LANCERS

James Ikin Nunnerley was born at Wilderspool in Warrington, Lancashire (now Cheshire) in 1830, the seventh son of Richard Nunnerley. He was apprenticed to a draper before he enlisted into the 17th Lancers in 1847. As a corporal he was on escort duty on 12 November 1852, for the funeral of the Duke of Wellington.

He saw active service in the East, where he was present at the battle of the Alma, and at Inkerman, and he took part in the Light Brigade action at Balaclava. He returned to the British lines without serious injury and he was promoted to sergeant on the following day. He received the Crimea Medal with *Alma, Balaclava, Inkerman* and *Sebastopol* clasps, the Turkish Medal, and the French War Medal was conferred to him in 1861, after taking his discharge in 1857.

He became station master on the railway at Disley near Stockport for two years, before moving to Ormskirk in Lancashire in 1859, where he became drill instructor to D Troop in Lord Lathom's Lancashire Hussars. He retired as Sergeant-Major in October 1881, and opened a drapery shop in Moor Street, Ormskirk.

He attended the Balaclava reunion banquet in 1875, was a member of the Balaclava Commemoration Society, 1879, and he signed the Loyal Address in 1887. He was present at the Light Brigade benefit held in Manchester in 1890, and he was in Fleet Street for the Jubilee celebrations in 1897.

He attended the annual dinners of 1890, 1895 and 1897. A Meritorious Service Medal was presented to him by King Edward VII in 1904, and his medals are with the 17th/21st Lancers Museum in Grantham. He left an account of his military service in the form of a booklet entitled: *A Short Sketch of the 17th Lancers,* which was published at Liverpool in 1884, and at Ormskirk in 1890 and 1892.

Sergeant-Major Nunnerley died on 22 November 1905, aged seventy-five, and three days later the people of Ormskirk lined the streets to watch his military funeral as the cortege made its way to the Ormskirk Parish Churchyard for burial.

JOHN SMITH PARKINSON
11TH HUSSARS

John Parkinson was born in Grantham and was baptised there on 25 July 1835. He was the only child of Samuel Smith Parkinson, a commercial traveller (born 1811), and his wife, Ann (formerly Walter), who had married in Grantham on 14 July 1834. Sadly, his mother died in 1838 (December quarter), and his father married Mary Bugg (born 1816), in 1841 (June quarter).

John enlisted into the 11th Hussars at Nottingham in 1851, and embarked at Kingstown, Ireland, for service in the East, where he took part in the Light Brigade action at Balaclava. In 1906 an account by him in a Birmingham newspaper stated: 'So far as we could see then, there were about forty or fifty of us left, and Lord George Paget and Colonel Sewell agreed that the only alternative was to return to our starting point. We had been in the saddle since three o'clock in the morning without food or drink, and it was then between twelve and one o'clock in the day. The charge began about eleven. So exhausted were the horses, which had also started without breakfast, that many of them had to be literally beaten along with the sword sheaths.

As we approached the top of the valley we saw a troop of Lancers drawn up. The flags on their lances appeared to be white and red, and we at first took them for our own 17th Lancers. To our dismay, they proved to be Poles, placed there to bar our return, our supports having been late in arriving. It seemed certain that we would be annihilated, for besides being outnumbered - we were exhausted. We made a dash for it, and though I found afterwards I had been pricked slightly by a lance in the back of the neck, I cannot tell quite how I came by it, and certainly the majority of the Poles allowed us to pass without showing fight. Nearly all of us got through, whereas the Poles could have wiped us out.'

His mount had been shot under him and he had to catch a stray horse. His left leg was lacerated when a shell burst, and in all he was wounded in three places. His left boot was ruined and he had to tie his foot up with a piece of old sacking. He was invalided to Scutari later in the conflict. For his service in the East he received the Crimea Medal with four clasps, and the Turkish Medal.

He was promoted corporal in 1859, and sergeant in 1861. While he was stationed at Dublin, 1861-62, he formed a 'Corps Dramatique' within the regiment, and he acted as its stage manager. He left the Army at Dublin, on 10 June 1864.

Having married, he was employed with the South Eastern Railway Company at London Bridge until 1866, when he left London for family health reasons and became a mounted officer with the Birmingham Police Force. The greater part of his service was with B Division at Ladywood, and being promoted in 1869, he was sergeant in charge of the Ladywood police station. He retired from the police force in 1892, after twenty-six years. He had no army pension, but he received a superannuation, and help from the TH Roberts Fund.

John and Eliza lived at 6 Hick Street, Aston, Birmingham, where they had five children; Charlotte (born 1868); John (born 1870); William (born 1872); Annie (born 1874) and Ellen (born 1877). In 1881 they lived at 37 Alston Street, Birmingham, and by 1891 at 29 Common Hill Grove, King's Norton. Charlotte married Louis Trickett at King's Norton in 1884; Annie married George Dauncey at Solihull in 1899; and Ellen married Thomas Pearson in the Solihull registration district in 1906.

He was a member of the Balaclava Commemoration Society, and he signed the Loyal Address. He attended several reunion dinners, including the last one in 1913. He, and John Howes, were foremost in establishing the Birmingham Military Veterans' Association, and when the Balaclava Commemoration Society held their 189? reunion in Birmingham, Sergean? Parkinson took a leading part in its organisation.

Sergeant Parkinson was of a: 'retiring disposition', and it was said he: 'was a fine handsome figure, and his courtesy and gentlemanly conduct made him a favourite everywhere'. He spent much of his spare time working for the Association, and to raise funds he drew on his experience as a stage manager, and wearing a uniform of the 11th Hussars he attended social events to talk about his military life and recite Tennyson's famous poem. He is also believed to have accepted a music hall touring engagement.

King Edward VII and Queen Alexandra visited Birmingham in 1909, to open the new University. Sergeant Parkinson was in charge of an escort of veterans drawn-up outside the Town Hall. When the King stopped to inspect them he recognised Parkinson, and realised that the old soldier had taught him sword exercises in Dublin fifty years before.

The last years of his life were spent at 46 Bradford Road, Yardley. In January 1917, he was visiting his daughter, Annie Dauncey, at 125 Sandon Road, Edgbaston, when he caught pneumonia. He died on 12 January 1917, aged eighty-two. He was buried at Yardley Cemetery, Birmingham, with military honours, and among the estimated four thousand people who were present at his funeral were representatives of the 11th Hussars, the Birmingham Police Force, and the Birmingham Military Veterans' Association.

WILLIAM PEARSON
17TH LANCERS

William Pearson was born at Doncaster, on February 1825. He enlisted into the 17th Lancers, at the Royal Barracks, Dublin, on February 1848. He saw service in the East, being present at the battle of the Alma, and he took part in the Light Brigade action at Balaclava.

When the 17th Lancers reached the Russian guns they had ceased to exist as an effective unit, but small groups of men had rallied together, and among one of these was Private Pearson. He managed to break through the line of enemy Lancers, but three Cossacks moved in to try to cut him off. He gave reign to his charger, and with the momentum of his pace he succeeded in beating them off too. However, a fourth Cossack wheeled across his path and prepared to attack him. He had taught his horse to respond to certain gestures, and as he pressed his knees together the charger reared up, threatening the Cossack with its front legs, and forcing him to swerve away to miss the hoofs as they came down. He eventually broke free and spurred his horse on. Unfortunately, one of his assailants had stabbed him in the side with his lance, and although it did not trouble him at first, he eventually collapsed from severe pain and loss of blood. It was found that the lance had penetrated his lung.

Private Pearson was transported to the hospital at Scutari, where he suffered in dreadful conditions, and his chances of survival seemed slim until he was placed under the personal care of Florence Nightingale, who

even fitted him out with clothes for the journey back to England. However, due to rough conditions on board ship his health deteriorated, to such an extent that he opened his eyes one day to see two men trying on his boots and clothes, because they thought he was dead. He eventually came under the care of a doctor in Malta who 'patched me up and made me fit for service again.'

He was certified as only fit for depot duty and invalided on 7 December 1854. For his service in the East he received the Crimea Medal with *Alma, Balaclava* and *Sebastopol* clasps, and the Turkish Medal.

In 1857 the 'Devil's Wind' blew across northern India when religous fanaticism and opposition to British rule and modernisation caused unrest among the soldiers of the Bengal Army, which flared-up into widespread rebellion In early May, and a British force was sent to deal with the problem. Private Pearson had recovered from his wounds, and having retained his fighting spirit he volunteered for service.

He sailed with the regiment from Queenstown aboard the troopship *Great Britain*, and on arriving at Bombay the 17th Lancers joined the force being prepared by Sir Hugh Rose for service in Central India. It was an extremely difficult campaign, as they pursued leading rebels such as Tantia Topi. While on long forced marches they were under the constant threat of rebel attack and the ravages of disease, after which they assaulted large heavily-manned masonry fortresses. But they overcame these hardships and most of the rebel leaders were captured and executed. For his service Private Pearson received the Indian Mutiny Medal with *Central India* clasp.

He continued his service in India, where he discharged from the Army at Secunderabad in April 1860. His service record was described as 'very good', for which he received two 'good conduct' badges, and he also awarded the Long Service Good Conduct Medal.

On his return to England, William Pearson settled in York, making his home at 111 Walmgate, and gaining employment as turnkey at York Castle prison, where he freely admitted that he gave the lash to unruly inmates.

He attended the first Balaclava reunion banquet in 1875, was a member of the Balaclava Commemoration Society c 1879, he signed the Loyal Address in 1887 and he attended the Balaclava dinners i 1897 and 1908. He also benefitted from the TH Roberts Fund.

In later life William went to live with hi nephew, Sergeant George Toye, an ex Royal Marine, at 54 Monkgate, York. He i known to have enjoyed painting, and one o his pictures has survived and remains wit the family, along with his medals and som service papers. By 1909 William Pearson the last known survivor of the Ligh Brigade action at Balaclava living in York was in ill-health, and had begun to suffe severe attacks of bronchitis. Havin become bedridden, he died on 14 Jun 1909. He was aged eighty-four, and hi death was recorded as being caused b senile decay.

His funeral was attended by large number of local people and dignitaries, as he wa buried in York Cemetery (grave 554), wit military honours provided by the 5t Lancers and the Yorkshire Regimen (Green Howards). A local newspape report of the funeral recorded: 'Following came the gun carriage on which rested th coffin, covered with a Union Jack, and sur mounted by the deceased's busby and sword. The carriage was drawn by fou horses of the Army Service Corps, and fol lowing was a beautiful black horse whic was formerly with the 17th Lancers, and which was draped with a white cape. The deceased soldier's boots fixed feet upper most in the stirrups, as a symbol that he would ride no more.'

EDWARD SEAGER
8TH HUSSARS

The Seger family had lived in and around Liverpool for two hundred years, and many are buried in towns in the area. Edward Seger was born on 11 June 1812, of an old Speke family. On 23 October 1845 he married Jane Emily Rothwell, the daughter of an army captain, at St Lawrence's Church in York.

He had run away from home to join the army, his father twice having to pay to get him home. However, on the third occasion he changed his name to Seager: 'And his father could not do a thing.' On 29 November 1839, he became Regimental Sergeant-Major with the 8th Hussars, being promoted Cornet on 17 September 1841, and Lieutenant on 20 June 1843. He was Adjutant to the 8th Hussars from 3 October 1841 until 25 October 1854. He embarked for active service in the East, aboard the *Wilson Kennedy* on 2 May 1854. He took part in the Light Brigade action at Balaclava, where both he and his horse were wounded.

He described his experiences at Balaclava in one of the three hundred letters he wrote to his wife and family in Stretford, Manchester: 'You will hear that we were engaged with the enemy, and thank God, I have only received a slight wound on my right hand, and am obliged to write with my left. By some mistake the Light Brigade were ordered to attack the Russian Cavalry, and we had to proceed down the extent of a valley about a mile long, at the other end of which the Russians were posted in force, and on the hills on each side of the valley were posted the Russian guns, and also on our right a line of infantry armed with rifles. The whole of this force we had to pass before we got to their cavalry. We advanced in three lines, the 4th and 8th being the last line, sent in support. There were only about 100 of our regiment within the cross fire from both hills, both of cannon and rifles. The fire was tremendous, shells bursting amongst us, cannon balls tearing the earth up, Minie balls coming like hail. Still on we went, never altering our pace, or breaking us up in the least, except that our men and horses were gradually knocked over. Our men behaved nobly. I was riding in front of the men on the right of the line of officers. I then took command of the squadron, and placed myself in front of the centre. Malta, my mare, had just previously got a ball through her neck, just above the windpipe, but we went bravely on.

About this time we discovered a large body of Russian lancers coming on our rear to attack us. We immediately wheeled about to show fight. I kept with the squadron... in the front... leading. The men kept well together and bravely seconded us. We dashed at them, they were three deep, with lances levelled. I parried the first fellows lance, the one behind him I cut over the head, which no doubt he will remember for some time, and as I was recovering my sword, the third fellow made a tremendous point at my body. I had just time to receive his lance's point on the hilt of my sword, it got through the bow, knocked the skin off the knuckles of my second finger, coming out at the other side. I shall most likely be returned wounded.

We had to go back through the fire in a scattered manner so as not to give them so great a chance of killing us. On looking to see what had become of my men, I found they had got through and scattered to the left to get out of reach of the rifles, and a large body of lancers were coming on my left to cut us off. I put Malta to her speed and she soon got out of their reach, but the shot and rifle balls flew in great quantities. Shells bursting over my head with an awful crash. Through all the fire I returned, sometimes walking my horse, sometimes galloping, until I got out of reach of the fire and found the remainder of the regiment collecting gradually, and counting over the missing Many a poor fellow had laid low. Tha night I was glad to lie down and slept well.

He became captain on 26 October 1854 being appointed assistant military secretar to Major-General Lord William Paulet commanding on the Bosphorus, from 2 June 1855. He continued in this capacity t Sir Henry Storks until 31 July 1856. Fo his service he was awarded the Crime Medal with *Alma, Balaclava, Inkerman* an *Sebastopol* clasps, the Turkish Medal an the Order of Medjidie (5th Class).

He was promoted Major on 31 Januar 1858, serving in Central India under Hug Rose, for which he received the India Mutiny Medal with *Central India* clasp and he was mentioned in dispatches. H commanded the regiment for a period dur ing the early part of 1859, and he wa appointed Lieutenant-Colonel on 5 Augus 1859, and Brevet-Colonel on 5 Augus 1864. He served in Ireland, becoming Acting Quartermaster-General, Dubli District, from 3 November 1864 to 3 January 1870, being appointed Major General on 15 January 1870.

He received the Distinguished Conduc Medal on 10 May 1872. He attended th first Balaclava banquet in 1875. He serve as Inspecting Officer of Yeomanry Cavalr at York from 1 April 1873 to 3 April 1878 being appointed CB. He retired on 1 Jul 1881. General Seager died at Sion Hous in Scarborough, on 30 March 1883, aged seventy, and he was buried in th Smithdown Road Cemetery, Liverpool His family have his medals, sword, letters and parts of his uniform.

WILLIAM SEWELL
13TH *LIGHT DRAGOONS*

William Sewell was born at Dorking, Surrey, in May 1832, and enlisted into the 13th Light Dragoons at Westminster on 9 July 1851. He was five feet seven inches tall, with a fresh complexion, hazel eyes and brown hair. He sailed to the East with his regiment, where he took part in the Light Brigade action at Balaclava. He was severely wounded in the head, and when his horse was killed he had to mount a horse belonging to the enemy to get back to the British lines.

On his return to England he was presented before Queen Victoria at Brompton Barracks on 3 March 1855, and he was discharged at Chatham as unfit for further service, on 5 September 1855. He received the Crimea Medal with *Alma* and *Balaclava* clasps, and the Turkish Medal. As a result of his injury he wore a metal plate fixed over the wound for the rest of his life.

He settled in Liverpool, where he became coachman to the Earl family and married Mary, the cook. Their first child, Margaret, was born in 1857, and their second child, Helen, in 1860; but Margaret died when she was five. They moved to Woolton Hill, Liverpool, and William was for many years employed as coachman by Sir James Pickton. A son named William was born in 1868, but he died when he was aged three.

He was a member of the Balaclava Commemoration Society, and he was present at many reunions, his last one being at St James's Restaurant in London in 1906. William Sewell died at 18 Rose Lane, Mossley Hill, Liverpool, on 8 January 1910, aged seventy-eight. Edward Hindley attended the funeral, as he was buried at St Peter's Parish Church, Woolton, Liverpool. His wife died in 1907.

Survivors of the Light Brigade at a Balaclava reunion banquet.

GEORGE WILDE
4TH *LIGHT DRAGOONS*

George Wilde was born at St Margaret's parish, Norwich, in April 1825, where his father had become a Freeman of the City on 24 February 1819. George was a plasterer by trade, before he enlisted into the 4th Light Dragoons at Norwich, on 27 August 1842. He was aged eighteen years and five months, had a fair complexion, grey eyes and light brown hair.

He saw active service in the East, where he took part in the Light Brigade action at Balaclava. According to a Norwich newspaper: 'he rode in the front rank, had three horses killed under him, and was (slightly) wounded in the left arm.' He was promoted to corporal on 16 December 1855, and transferred to the 4th Battalion, Military Train, on 1 November 1856. He reverted to private at his own request on 1 July 1857. For his service he received the Crimea Medal with *Alma, Balaclava, Inkerman* and *Sebastopol* clasps, and the Turkish Medal.

He then saw active service during the Maori uprising in New Zealand, from 18 March 1863 to May 1864, for which he wore the New Zealand Medal, and he also received the Long Service Good Conduct Medal.

He discharged from the army at the Royal Victoria Hospital, Netley, on 26 February 1867, as: 'Unfit for further service due to chronic rheumatism. The result of long service and exposure. Has broken-down constitution which will materially affect his ability to earn his livelihood.' He was awarded a pension of thirteen pence a day. He had served in the army for twenty-four years, his conduct was described as 'exemplary', and he was in possession of four good conduct badges.

He returned to Norwich, where he lived with his wife, Mary, at 35 Gladstone Road, Heigham, Norwich. He was made Freeman of the City like his father before him, on 2 October 1868. He had a daughter who married William Fox, and by 1881 their daughter, Mary, was living with her grand-parents. He became well-known in the city described as: 'a steady hard-working man'. He was Seargeant-at-Arms to the Norwich parliament, and he was employed as a porter and general attendant at the YMCA in St Giles. Towards the end of his life he became a member of the Uthanks Road Methodist Church.

He attended the Balaclava Reunion Banquet in 1875, and he was a member of the Commemoration Society, 1879. He was present at the funeral of Frederick Armes in 1885, whose death made him the last known survivor of the Light Brigade action in Norwich.

George Wilde died at his home on 18 May 1887, aged sixty-two, from 'atrophy of the liver.' William Fox was with him and is the informant on the death certificate. He was buried in the Rosary Cemetery in Norwich (section 1/A, grave 125). There is a weather-worn headstone. His medals are in the keep at Norwich Castle Museum.

RICHARD HALL WILLIAMS
17TH LANCERS

Richard Hall Williams was born in the parish of St James's, Bath, in August 1821, and he was a compositor by trade. When his family moved to Lancashire, he began his working life as a booking clerk at Worsley railway station, before he enlisted into the 17th Lancers in London on 15 November 1843.

He saw active service in the East, where he took part in the Light Brigade action at Balaclava. He had a severe abscess on his nose at the time and had to wear a blood-stained bandage around his face to protect it. 'My visage was so fearsome that the Russians held their fire. But the pain was such that the following day I must report to the regimental surgeon; a step not taken lightly in the regiment. Two orderlies hold me and I receive a smart buffet on the nose which disperses the fluid.' Apart from a slight case of cholera', he came back from the campaign without serious injury, having been promoted to Troop Sergeant-Major on the first day of 1855. For his service he was awarded the Crimea Medal with *Alma, Balaclava, Inkerman* and *Sebastopol* clasps, and the Turkish Medal.

He spent nine years in India from 1857, taking part in several engagements throughout the country. He received the Indian Mutiny Medal with *Central India* clasp. He was also presented with a Long Service Good Conduct Medal, and a Meritorious Service Medal. His medals are now in a private collection. He discharged from the Army at Brighton, on 10 November 1867, and as a

token of regard from his comrades in arms he was presented with a commemorative silver drinking cup.

He took up residence with his family in a house at Clifton Road, Eccles, near Manchester, and in about 1870 he became post-master at the Worsley village post office. He became Troop Sergeant-Major with the Worsley Troop of the Duke of Lancaster's Own Yeomanry, taking drill with them in the meadow behind his home. He is said to have had a passion for performing drill movements to the beat of music on horseback, dismounted and with the sabre. He retired from the Yeomanry in 1877, having been given permission to carry on his duties for eight years beyond the regulation time. He was presented with a sword of honour which is inscribed: 'A token of esteem and respect for his uniform conduct as a soldier and a gentleman.' He kept himself busy by teaching drill and deportment to the children of the Earl of Ellesmere until 1893. Tragically, his own first child, Richard, died a teenager in 1885.

A 'highly respected member of the community', he and his wife, Fanny Jane, worshipped at the Worsley Parish Church, and they and all their children became involved with the church in various capacities. A note in the parish magazine at the time of his death stated: 'He used to recite Tennyson's poem The Charge of the Light Brigade at tea parties and concerts - putting it over with feeling, because he was there.'

Introduced into Freemasonry at Colchester in 1857, he was one of the founder members of the Worsley Lodge, of which the Earl of Ellesmere was the first Master. He was a member of the Balaclava Commemoration Society, and he signed the Loyal Address. He attended a benefit concert at the Free Trade Hall in Manchester on 21 May 1890 to raise funds for survivors of the Light Brigade who were living in the north of England, and he travelled to Fleet Street for the Jubilee celebrations. He attended several reunions, his last one being in 1908.

Sergeant-Major Williams died on 7 July 1910, aged ninety-one. He was buried with military honours at St Mark's Parish Church, Worsley There was a large presence of Freemasons at his funeral, and a wreath was received from TH Roberts. He left a widow and five children.

The programme for the service of thanksgiving held at Worsley in 2004, to commemorate the 150th anniversary of the Charge.

In 1967, his surviving son, Clement, presented his father's silver cup to the Worsley Freemasons, to be used by each reigning Master. Clement died in 1974, in his one hundredth year. The sword of honour is now in the Lancashire County and Regimental Museum at Preston.

on 20 October 2004, I attended a service of remembrance to mark the 150th anniversary of the Light Brigade action held at the Worsley parish church. The church bell tolled one hundred and eighteen times to mark the number of men said to have been killed in the action.

THOMAS WILLIAMS
17TH LANCERS

Thomas Williams was born in Leeds in 1830, the son of William James Williams and his wife, Sarah. He was a labourer prior to his enlistment into the 11th Hussars in June 1850, to serve alongside his older brother, James, who was also born in Leeds, and had enlisted into the 11th Hussars on 30 January 1831. At the time of the Crimean War they were both serving in G Troop, where they were known as Old Taffy and Young Taffy because of their age difference and their surname being of Welsh origin.

James and Thomas were posted to serve in the East, where they were present at the battle of the Alma on 20 September 1854, and they took part in the Light Brigade action at Balaclava. James had been promoted to corporal. He was wounded during the action, which hindered his ability to get back to the British lines, and during the hand-to-hand fighting he was captured by the enemy and marched into Russia as a prisoner of war. Several eye-witness accounts reported how the British behaved with great courage and dignity while in the hands of the Russians, and James died of his wounds while he was in captivity.

Thomas got back to the British lines without serious injury to learn that his brother had been reported missing, and he was never to see him again. He was present at the battle of Inkerman on 5 November 1854, and service papers show that he was on letter duty in April 1855. For his service, Private Williams was awarded the Crimea Medal with *Alma, Balaclava, Inkerman* and *Sebastopol* clasps, and the Turkish Medal. They are held in an English private collection.

Possibly due to his terrible experiences in the Crimea, and in particular the loss of his brother, Thomas discharged from the Army soon after returning to Britain. He went to live with his family at 36 Clint Road, off Durning Road, Wavertree, Liverpool 7.

Thomas Williams attended the Balaclava reunion banquet at the Alexandra Palace in London, on the Twenty-first anniversary of the battle. He was accompanied by William J Williams, who was originally thought to be James Williams. However, this person was probably their father 'representing' his son. The name William J Williams appears on the 1877 list of members of the Balaclava Commemoration Society, but not on the revised list made in 1879, when individuals had to prove that they had been present at the battle, and the committee may have discovered his true identity. Thomas became a member of the Commemoration Society in 1879, and he signed the Loyal Address in 1887.

Thomas Williams died on 19 May 1887, aged fifty-seven, and he was buried with his mother at St Mary's Churchyard, Mount Vernon Street, Edge Hill, Liverpool 7. A memorial stone was erected at the grave which states that he was 'One of the Balaclava Heroes.'

THOMAS WRIGHT
17TH LANCERS

Thomas Wright was born at Warrington, on 3 December 1830, and enlisted into the 17th Lancers on the day after his twenty-first birthday in 1851. He saw active service in the East, and he took part in the Light Brigade action at Balaclava, where his horse was shot under him, and, when a fellow 17th Lancer requested his assistance he is reported to have replied: 'It is every man for himself today'. For his service he received the Crimea Medal with *Alma, Balaclava, Inkerman* and *Sebastopol* clasps, and the Turkish Medal.

He served in the Indian Mutiny in 1858, as servant to Major Curzon, and when the major offered to pay the twenty pounds for him to leave the Army and work for him in Leicestershire, he accepted, and discharged at Secunderabad in 1861, having served over nine years. He returned home on the *Norwood*. He received the Indian Mutiny Medal with *Central India* clasp, and a Good Conduct badge.

He remained in Major Curzon's employ until becoming a Warden at Maidstone Prison. After eighteen months he returned to Warrington, then moved to Luton Street, Widnes. He was illiterate, but he got by doing labouring work about the town, and odd jobs at the local Police Station. By 1896 his health was deteriorating and prevented him from working, and he was granted a pension of one shilling a day from the Royal Patriotic Fund. This pension was stopped when he gained employment as a night watchman, but he lost that job and was forced to pawn his medals. The pension was eventually reinstated. He signed the Loyal Address, and he was invited to London for the Jubilee celebration, and he is believed to have been at four other reunions. He was granted ten shillings a week from the T H Roberts Fund, and was able to retrieve his medals out of pawn.

'Old Tom' suffered a stroke in May 1902 which left him paralysed, and he died on 15 May 1902, at 29 Major Cross Street, Widnes. He was aged seventy-one, and had never married. His coat bearing his medals was draped over the coffin at his funeral. He was buried in Farnworth Cemetery, Widnes, and a memorial stone at the grave was paid for by public subscription.